新丝路"中文+职业技能"系列教材编写委员会
（中文+物流管理）

总策划：马箭飞　谢永华

策　划：邵旭波　邵亦鹏　张海宁

顾　问：朱志平（北京师范大学）

　　　　林秀琴（首都师范大学）

　　　　宋继华（北京师范大学）

总主编：谢永华　杜曾慧

语言类主编：易　华

专业类主编：谈　慧

语言类副主编：周　波　史其慧

专业类副主编：张　瑜　周立军　王桂花

项目组长：郭凤岚

项目副组长：付彦白

项目成员：郭　冰　武传霞　齐　琰　赫　栗　李金梅

新丝路"中文+职业技能"系列教材
New Silk Road "Chinese + Vocational Skills" Series

中文+物流管理
Chinese + Logistics Management

中级 Intermediate

新丝路"中文+职业技能"系列教材编写委员会 编

© 2023 北京语言大学出版社，社图号 23247

图书在版编目（CIP）数据

中文＋物流管理．中级 ／ 新丝路"中文＋职业技能"系列教材编写委员会编．－－北京：北京语言大学出版社，2023.12

新丝路"中文＋职业技能"系列教材
ISBN 978-7-5619-6462-0

Ⅰ．①中… Ⅱ．①新… Ⅲ．①汉语－对外汉语教学－教材②物流管理－教材　Ⅳ．① H195.4 ② F252.1

中国国家版本馆 CIP 数据核字（2023）第 236075 号

中文＋物流管理（中级）
ZHONGWEN + WULIU GUANLI (ZHONGJI)

排版制作：	北京创艺涵文化发展有限公司
责任印制：	周　燚

出版发行：	北京语言大学出版社
社　　址：	北京市海淀区学院路 15 号，100083
网　　址：	www.blcup.com
电子信箱：	service@blcup.com
电　　话：	编 辑 部　8610-82303647/3592/3395
	国内发行　8610-82303650/3591/3648
	海外发行　8610-82303365/3080/3668
	北语书店　8610-82303653
	网购咨询　8610-82303908
印　　刷：	北京富资园科技发展有限公司

版　次：	2023 年 12 月第 1 版	印　次：	2023 年 12 月第 1 次印刷
开　本：	889 毫米 × 1194 毫米 1/16	印　张：	9.5
字　数：	170 千字		
定　价：	98.00 元		

PRINTED IN CHINA

凡有印装质量问题，本社负责调换。售后 QQ 号 1367565611，电话 010-82303590

编写说明

新丝路"中文＋职业技能"系列教材是把中文作为第二语言，结合专业和职业的专门用途、职业用途的中文教材，不是专业理论教材，不是一般意义的通用综合中文教材。本系列教材定位为职场生存中文教材、立体式技能型语言教材。教材研发的目标是既要满足学习者一般中文环境下的基本交际需求，又要满足学习者职业学习需求和职场工作需求。它和普通的国际中文教材的区别不在语法，而在词汇的专门化程度，在中文的用途、使用场合、应用范围。目前，专门用途、职业用途的中文教材在语言分类和研究成果上几近空白，本系列教材的成功研发开创了中文学习的新视野、新领域、新方向，将"中文＋职业技能＋X等级证书"真正融合，使学习者在学习中文的同时，也可通过实践掌握职业技能，从而获得X等级证书。

适用对象

本系列教材将适用对象定位为双零基础（零语言基础、零技能基础）的来华学习中文和先进技能的长期或者短期进修生，可满足初、中、高各层次专业课程的教学需要。教材亦可供海内外相关的培训课程及"走出去"的中资企业培训本土化员工使用。

结构规模

本系列教材采取专项语言技能与职业技能训练相结合的中文教学及教材编写模式。教材选择当前热门的物流管理、汽车服务工程技术、电子商务、机电一体化、计算机网络技术、酒店管理等六个专业，培养各专业急需急用的技术岗位人才。每个专业教材均包括初、中、高级三册。每一册都配有专业视频教学资源，还附有"视频脚本""参考答案"等配套资源。

编写理念

本系列教材将词语进行分类，区分普通词语和专业词语，以通用语料为基础，以概念性、行为性词语为主，不脱离职场情境讨论分级，做到控制词汇量，控制工作场景，控制交流内容与方式，构建语义框架。将语言的分级和专业的分级科学地融合，是实现本系列教材成功编写的关键。

教材目标

语言技能目标：

初级阶段，能熟练掌握基础通用词语和职场的常用专业词语，能使用简短句子进行简单的生活及工作交流。中级阶段，能听懂工作场合简单的交谈与发言，明白大意，把握基本情况，能就工作中重要的话题用简单的话与人沟通。高级阶段，能听懂工作场合一般的交谈与发言，抓住主要内容和关键信息，使用基本交际策略与人交流、开展工作，能初步了解与交际活动相关的文化因素，掌握与交际有关的一般文化背景知识，能排除交际时遇到的文化障碍。交际能力层次的递进实现从初级的常规礼节、基本生活及工作的交流能力，到中级的简单的服务流程信息交流能力，最后达到高级的复杂信息的交流和特情处理的能力。

职业技能目标：

以满足岗位需求为目标，将遴选出的当前热门的专业工作岗位分为初、中、高三级。物流管理专业初、中、高级对应的岗位分别是物流员、物流经理、物流总监；汽车服务工程技术专业初、中、高级对应的岗位分别是汽车机电维修工、汽车服务顾问、技术总监；电子商务专业初、中、高级对应的岗位分别是电子商务运营助理、电子商务运营员、电子商务客服；机电一体化专业初、中、高级对应的岗位分别是机电操作工、机电调整工、机电维修工；计算机网络技术专业初、中、高级对应的岗位分别是宽带运维工程师、网络运维专员、网络管理员；酒店管理专业初、中、高级对应的岗位分别是前厅基层接待员、前厅主管、前厅经理。每个专业分解出三十个工作场景/任务，学习者在学习后能够全面掌握此岗位的概况及基本程序，实现语言学习和专业操作的双重目标。

编写原则

1. 语言知识技能与专业知识技能并进，满足当前热门的、急需急用的岗位需求。

2. 渐进分化，综合贯通，拆解难点，分而治之。

3. 语言知识与专业知识科学、高效复现，语言技能与专业技能螺旋式上升，职场情境、语义框架、本体输入方式相互配合。

4. 使用大量的图片和视频，实现专业知识和技能呈现形式可视化。

5. 强化专业岗位实操性技能。本系列教材配有专业技术教学的视频，突出展示专业岗位的实操性技能，语言学习难度与技能掌握难度的不匹配可通过实操性强的视频和实训环节来补充。

特色追求

本系列教材从初级最基础的语音知识学习和岗位认知开始，将"中文＋职业技能"融入在工作场景对话中，把工作分解成一个个任务，用图片认知的方式解决专业词语的认知问题，用视频展示的方法解决学习者掌握中文词语与专业技能的不匹配问题，注重技能的实操性，注重"在做中学"。每一单元都设置了"学以致用"板块，目的不仅仅是解决本单元任务的词语认知问题，更是将学习的目标放在"能听""能用""能模仿说出"上。我们力争通过大量图片的使用和配套视频的展示，将教材打造成立体式、技能型语言教材，方便学习者能够更好地自主学习。

使用建议

1. 本系列教材每个专业分为初、中、高级三册，每册10单元，初级每单元建议8～10课时完成，中级10～12课时完成，高级12～14课时完成。

2. 教材注释和说明着力于简明扼要，注重实操性，注重听说技能培养，对于教材涉及的语法知识，教师可视情况予以细化和补充。

3. "单元实训"板块可以在课文和语言点学完之后作为课堂练习使用，建议2课时完成。教师要带着学习者按照实训步骤一步步完成，实训步骤不要求学习者能够看懂，读懂，重要的是教师要引领操作，实现学习者掌握专业技能的目标。

4. "单元小结"板块是对整个单元关键词语和核心内容的总结，对于这部分内容，教师要进行听说练习，以便更好地帮助学习者了解本单元的核心工作任务。

5. 教师上课时要充分利用教材设计的练习，引导学习者多听多练，听说结合，学做合一。

6. 教师要带着学习者熟练诵读课文，要求学习者把每课的关键词语和句子、课堂用语背诵下来。

特别感谢

感谢教育部中外语言交流合作中心将新丝路"中文＋职业技能"系列教材列为重点研发项目，为我们教材编写增添了动力和责任感。教材编写委员会负责整套教材的规划、设计与编写协调，并先后召开上百次讨论会，对每册教材的课文编写、体例安排、注释说明、练习设计、图片选择、视频制作等进行全方位的评估、讨论和审定。感谢编写委员会成员和所有编者高度的敬业精神、精益求精的编写态度，以及所投入的热情和精力、付出的心血与智慧。感谢关注本系列教材并贡献宝贵意见的国际中文教育教学界专家和全国各地的同人。

新丝路"中文＋职业技能"系列教材编写委员会

2023年4月

Compilation Instructions

The New Silk Road "Chinese + Vocational Skills" is a series of Chinese textbooks for specialized and vocational purposes that combine professional and vocational technologies with Chinese as a second language. Instead of being specialized theoretical textbooks, or comprehensive or universal Chinese textbooks in a general sense, this series is intended to be Chinese textbooks for career survival, and three-dimensional skills-based language textbooks. The textbooks are developed with a view to meeting students' basic communication needs in general Chinese environment, and their professional learning needs and workplace demands as well. They are different from ordinary Chinese textbooks for foreigners in the degree of specialization of vocabulary, in the purpose, usage occasion, and application scope of Chinese (not in grammar). At present, Chinese textbooks for specialized and vocational purposes are virtually non-existent in terms of language classification and research results, so the successful development of this series has opened up new horizons, new fields and new directions for Chinese learning, and virtually integrated "Chinese + Vocational Skills + X-Level Certificates", which enables students to practically master vocational skills and obtain X-level certificates while learning Chinese.

Applicable Targets

This series is targeted at long-term or short-term students who come to China to learn Chinese and advanced skills with zero language basis and zero skill basis, which can meet the teaching needs of the elementary, intermediate and advanced specialized courses. This series can also be used for relevant training courses at home and abroad and for Chinese-funded enterprises that "go global" to train local employees.

Structure and Scale

This series adopts a Chinese teaching and textbook compilation model combining special language skills and vocational skills training. The series includes the textbooks for six popular majors such as logistics management, automotive service engineering technology, e-commerce, mechatronics, computer networking technology, and hotel management to cultivate technical talents in urgent need. The textbooks for each major consist of the textbooks at the elementary, intermediate and advanced levels. Each textbook is equipped with professional video teaching resources, and "video scripts", "reference answers" and other supporting resources as well.

Compilation Concept

This series classifies the vocabulary into general vocabulary and specialized vocabulary. Based on the general vocabulary, it focuses on conceptual and behavioral words, not deviating from workplace situations, so as to control the vocabulary, work scenarios and content and means of communication, and build the semantic framework. The scientific integration of language classification and specialty classification is the key to the successful compilation of textbooks.

Textbook Objectives

Language Skill Objectives

For students at the elementary level, they are trained to be familiar with basic general vocabulary and common specialized vocabulary in the workplace, and be able to use short sentences for simple communication in life and at work. For those at the intermediate level, they are trained to understand simple conversations and speeches in the workplace, comprehend the main ideas, grasp the basic situations, and communicate with others in simple words on important topics at work. For those at the advanced level, they are trained to be able to understand general conversations and speeches in the workplace, grasp the main content and key information, use basic communication strategies to communicate with others and carry out the work, have a preliminary understanding of cultural factors related to communication activities, master the general communication-related cultural background knowledge, and overcome cultural barriers encountered during communication. The progression in level of communicative competence helps them to leap forward from routine etiquette, basic communication in life and at work at the elementary level, to simple information exchange of service processes at the intermediate level, and finally to complex information exchange and handling of special circumstances at the advanced level.

Vocational Skill Objectives

To meet job requirements at the elementary, intermediate and advanced levels, the professional positions that are most urgently needed overseas are selected. The positions corresponding to logistics management at the elementary, intermediate and advanced levels are logistics staff, logistics managers and logistics directors; the positions corresponding to automotive service engineering technology at the elementary, intermediate and advanced levels are automotive electromechanical maintenance staff, automotive service consultants and technical directors; the positions corresponding to e-commerce at the elementary, intermediate and advanced levels are electronic operation assistants, e-commerce operators and e-commerce customer service staff; the positions corresponding to mechatronics at the elementary, intermediate and advanced levels are mechanical and electrical operators, mechanical and electrical adjusters, and mechanical and electrical maintenance staff; the positions corresponding to computer networking techology at the elementary, intermediate and advanced levels are broadband operation and maintenance engineers, network operation and maintenance specialists, and network administrators; the positions corresponding to hotel management at the elementary, intermediate and advanced levels are lobby receptionists, lobby supervisors and lobby managers. Through 30 work scenarios/tasks set for each major, learners can fully grasp the general situations and basic procedures of the position after learning, and achieve the dual goals of language learning and professional operation.

Principles of Compilation

1. Language knowledge skills and professional knowledge skills go hand in hand to meet the demands of current popular and urgently needed job positions;

2. It makes progressive differentiation and comprehensive integration, breaking down, dividing and conquering difficult points;

3. Language knowledge and professional knowledge recur scientifically and efficiently, language skills and professional skills spiral upward, and the situational stage, semantic framework, and ontology input methods cooperate with each other;

4. Professional knowledge and skills are visualized, using a lot of pictures and videos;

5. It strengthens the practical skills in professional positions. This series of textbooks is equipped with videos of professional technical training, highlighting the practical skills for professional positions. It addresses the mismatch between the difficulty of language learning and that of mastering skills by supplementing with practical videos and practical training.

Characteristic Pursuit

Starting from the basic phonetic knowledge learning and job cognition at the elementary level, this series integrates "Chinese + Vocational Skills" into the working scene dialogues, breaking down the job into various tasks, solving lexical students' problems by means of picture cognition, solving the problem of the mismatch between students' mastery of Chinese vocabulary and professional skills by means of displaying videos, stressing the practicality of skills, and focusing on "learning by doing". Each unit has a "Practicing What You Have Learnt" module, which not only solves the problem of lexical cognition of this unit, but also takes "being able to comprehend", "being able to use" and "being able to imitate" as the learning objectives. We strive to use a large number of pictures and display supporting videos to build the textbooks into three-dimensional skills-based language teaching materials, so that learners can learn more independently.

Recommendations for Use

1. Each major of this series consists of three volumes at the elementary, intermediate, and advanced levels, with 10 units in each volume. For each unit, it is recommended to be completed in 8-10 class hours at the elementary level, 10-12 class hours at the intermediate level, and 12-14 class hours at the advanced level.

2. The notes and explanations in the textbooks focus on conciseness, practicality, and the training of listening and speaking skills. The grammar knowledge in the textbooks can be detailed and supplemented by teachers as the case may be.

3. "Unit Practical Training" module can be used as a classroom exercise after the texts and language points, preferably to be completed in two class hours. Teachers should guide students to complete the training tasks step by step. Students are not required to read and understand the training steps. It is important that teachers guide students to achieve the goal of mastering professional skills.

4. "Unit Summary" module summarizes the keywords and core content of the entire unit. Through listening and speaking exercises, this part can better help learners understand the core tasks of this unit.

5. Teachers should make full use of the exercises designed in the textbooks during class, and guide students to listen more and practice more, combine listening and speaking, and integrate learning with practice.

6. Teachers should guide students to proficiently read the texts aloud, asking them to recite the keywords, sentences and classroom expressions in each unit.

Acknowledgements

We are grateful to the Center for Language Education and Cooperation of the Ministry of Education for listing the New Silk Road "Chinese + Vocational Skills" series as a key research and development project, which adds motivation and a sense of responsibility to our textbook compilation. The Textbook Compilation Committee is responsible for the planning, design, compilation and coordination of the entire set of textbooks, and has held hundreds of seminars to conduct a comprehensive evaluation, discussion, examination and approval of text compilation, style arrangement, notes and explanations, exercise design, picture selection, and video production of each textbook. We are indebted to the members of the Compilation Committee and all compilers for their professional dedication, unwavering pursuit of perfection in the compilation, as well as their enthusiasm, hard work and wisdom. We are thankful to the experts in international Chinese language education and colleagues from all over the country who have kept a close eye on this series and contributed their valuable opinions.

Compilation Committee of New Silk Road "Chinese + Vocational Skills" Series

April 2023

rénwù jièshào
人物介绍
Characters Introduction

cāngkù zǔzhǎng
仓库 组长
warehouse team leader

dìngdān zǔzhǎng
订单 组长
order team leader

dìngdānyuán
订单员
information clerk

cāngkù bǎoguǎnyuán (cāngguǎnyuán)
仓库 保管员（仓管员）
warehouse keeper

bāozhuāngyuán
包装员
packager

jiǎnhuòyuán
拣货员
sorter

bāozhuāng zǔzhǎng
包装 组长
packaging team leader

jiǎnhuò zǔzhǎng
拣货 组长
picking team leader

yùnshūyuán
运输员
deliverer

yùnshū zǔzhǎng
运输 组长
transportation team leader

9

语法术语及缩略形式参照表
Abbreviations of Grammar Terms

Grammar Terms in Chinese	Grammar Terms in Pinyin	Grammar Terms in English	Abbreviations
名词	míngcí	noun	n.
专有名词	zhuānyǒu míngcí	proper noun	pn.
代词	dàicí	pronoun	pron.
数词	shùcí	numeral	num.
量词	liàngcí	measure word	m.
数量词	shùliàngcí	quantifier	q.
动词	dòngcí	verb	v.
助动词	zhùdòngcí	auxiliary	aux.
形容词	xíngróngcí	adjective	adj.
副词	fùcí	adverb	adv.
介词	jiècí	preposition	prep.
连词	liáncí	conjunction	conj.
助词	zhùcí	particle	part.
拟声词	nǐshēngcí	onomatopoeia	onom.
叹词	tàncí	interjection	int.
前缀	qiánzhuì	prefix	pref.
后缀	hòuzhuì	suffix	suf.
成语	chéngyǔ	idiom	idm.
短语	duǎnyǔ	phrase	phr.
主语	zhǔyǔ	subject	S
谓语	wèiyǔ	predicate	P
宾语	bīnyǔ	object	O
定语	dìngyǔ	attributive	Attrib
状语	zhuàngyǔ	adverbial	Adverb
补语	bǔyǔ	complement	C

CONTENTS 目 录

第一单元　订单处理　Unit 1　Order Processing　　1

第一部分　课文　**Texts**　　2
　　一、热身 Warm-up　　2
　　二、课文 Texts　　4
　　三、视听说 Viewing, Listening and Speaking　　6
　　四、学以致用 Practicing What You Have Learnt　　6
　　五、小知识 Tips　　8

第二部分　汉字　**Chinese Characters**　　8
　　一、汉字知识 Knowledge about Chinese Characters　　8
　　　　1. 汉字的笔画（1） Strokes of Chinese characters (1)
　　　　　　一　丨　丿　乀
　　　　2. 汉字的笔顺（1） Stroke orders of Chinese characters (1)
　　　　　　先横后竖 Horizontal strokes before vertical strokes
　　　　　　先撇后捺 Left-falling strokes before right-falling strokes
　　二、汉字认读与书写 The Recognition and Writing of Chinese Characters　　9

第三部分　日常用语　**Daily Expressions**　　9

第四部分　单元实训　**Unit Practical Training**　　9
　　订单处理实训 Practical Training of Order Processing　　9

第五部分　单元小结　**Unit Summary**　　10

第二单元　流通加工　Unit 2　Distribution Processing　　13

第一部分　课文　**Texts**　　14
　　一、热身 Warm-up　　14
　　二、课文 Texts　　16
　　三、视听说 Viewing, Listening and Speaking　　19
　　四、学以致用 Practicing What You Have Learnt　　20
　　五、小知识 Tips　　21

I

第二部分 汉字 **Chinese Characters** 21
    一、汉字知识 Knowledge about Chinese Characters 21
        1. 汉字的笔画（2） Strokes of Chinese characters (2)
        丶 乛 乚 ㇏
        2. 汉字的笔顺（2） Stroke orders of Chinese characters (2)
        先上后下 Upper strokes before lower strokes
        先左后右 Left-side strokes before right-side strokes
    二、汉字认读与书写 The Recognition and Writing of Chinese Characters 22
第三部分 日常用语 **Daily Expressions** 22
第四部分 单元实训 **Unit Practical Training** 22
    流通加工应用实训 Practical Training of Distribution Processing Application 22
第五部分 单元小结 **Unit Summary** 23

第三单元　摘果式拣选　Unit 3　DPS Picking　25

第一部分 课文 **Texts** 26
    一、热身 Warm-up 26
    二、课文 Texts 28
    三、视听说 Viewing, Listening and Speaking 30
    四、学以致用 Practicing What You Have Learnt 31
    五、小知识 Tips 32
第二部分 汉字 **Chinese Characters** 32
    一、汉字知识 Knowledge about Chinese Characters 32
        1. 汉字的笔画（3） Strokes of Chinese characters (3)
        ⺄ 亅 ㇀ ㇄
        2. 汉字的笔顺（3） Stroke orders of Chinese characters (3)
        先中间后两边 Strokes in the middle before those on both sides
        先外边后里边 Outside strokes before inside strokes
    二、汉字认读与书写 The Recognition and Writing of Chinese Characters 33
第三部分 日常用语 **Daily Expressions** 33
第四部分 单元实训 **Unit Practical Training** 33
    摘果式拣选应用实训 Practical Training of DPS Picking Application 33
第五部分 单元小结 **Unit Summary** 34

第四单元　播种式拣选　Unit 4　DAS Picking　37

第一部分　课文　**Texts**　38
　　一、热身 Warm-up　38
　　二、课文 Texts　40
　　三、视听说 Viewing, Listening and Speaking　42
　　四、学以致用 Practicing What You Have Learnt　42
　　五、小知识 Tips　43

第二部分　汉字　**Chinese Characters**　44
　　一、汉字知识 Knowledge about Chinese Characters　44
　　　　1. 汉字的笔画（4）　Strokes of Chinese characters (4)
　　　　　㇔ 丨 亅 乀
　　　　2. 汉字的笔顺（4）　Stroke orders of Chinese characters (4)
　　　　　先外后里再封口 Outside strokes before inside strokes, and then sealing strokes
　　二、汉字认读与书写 The Recognition and Writing of Chinese Characters　44

第三部分　日常用语　**Daily Expressions**　45

第四部分　单元实训　**Unit Practical Training**　45
　　播种式拣选应用实训 Practical Training of DAS Picking Application　45

第五部分　单元小结　**Unit Summary**　46

第五单元　补货作业　Unit 5　Replenishment Operation　49

第一部分　课文　**Texts**　50
　　一、热身 Warm-up　50
　　二、课文 Texts　51
　　三、视听说 Viewing, Listening and Speaking　53
　　四、学以致用 Practicing What You Have Learnt　54
　　五、小知识 Tips　55

第二部分　汉字　**Chinese Characters**　55
　　一、汉字知识 Knowledge about Chinese Characters　55
　　　　1. 汉字的笔画（5）　Strokes of Chinese characters (5)
　　　　　乚 ㇠ 𠃍 乙
　　　　2. 汉字的结构（1）　Structures of Chinese characters (1)
　　　　　独体结构 Independent structure
　　二、汉字认读与书写 The Recognition and Writing of Chinese Characters　56

第三部分　日常用语　**Daily Expressions**　56

第四部分　单元实训　**Unit Practical Training**　56
　　补货作业应用实训 Practical Training of Replenishment Operation Application　56

第五部分　单元小结　**Unit Summary**　57

III

第六单元　配装作业　Unit 6　Loading Operation　59

第一部分　课文　**Texts**　60
　　一、热身 Warm-up　60
　　二、课文 Texts　62
　　三、视听说 Viewing, Listening and Speaking　64
　　四、学以致用 Practicing What You Have Learnt　65
　　五、小知识 Tips　65

第二部分　汉字　**Chinese Characters**　66
　　一、汉字知识 Knowledge about Chinese Characters　66
　　　　1. 汉字的笔画（6）　Strokes of Chinese characters (6)
　　　　　　㇉ ㇌
　　　　2. 汉字的结构（2）　Structures of Chinese characters (2)
　　　　　　品字形结构　品-shaped structure
　　二、汉字认读与书写 The Recognition and Writing of Chinese Characters　66

第三部分　日常用语　**Daily Expressions**　66

第四部分　单元实训　**Unit Practical Training**　67
　　配装作业应用实训 Practical Training of Loading Operation Application　67

第五部分　单元小结　**Unit Summary**　67

第七单元　退货作业　Unit 7　Return Operation　69

第一部分　课文　**Texts**　70
　　一、热身 Warm-up　70
　　二、课文 Texts　72
　　三、视听说 Viewing, Listening and Speaking　73
　　四、学以致用 Practicing What You Have Learnt　74
　　五、小知识 Tips　75

第二部分　汉字　**Chinese Characters**　75
　　一、汉字知识 Knowledge about Chinese Characters　75
　　　　1. 汉字的笔画（7）　Strokes of Chinese characters (7)
　　　　　　㇆ ㇂
　　　　2. 汉字的结构（3）　Structures of Chinese characters (3)
　　　　　　上下结构　Top-bottom structure
　　　　　　上中下结构　Top-middle-bottom structure
　　二、汉字认读与书写 The Recognition and Writing of Chinese Characters　76

第三部分 日常用语	**Daily Expressions**	76
第四部分 单元实训	**Unit Practical Training**	76
退货作业应用实训 Practical Training of Return Operation Application		76
第五部分 单元小结	**Unit Summary**	77

第八单元　运输调度　Unit 8　Transportation Scheduling　79

第一部分　课文　**Texts**　80
　　一、热身 Warm-up　80
　　二、课文 Texts　82
　　三、视听说 Viewing, Listening and Speaking　84
　　四、学以致用 Practicing What You Have Learnt　85
　　五、小知识 Tips　85

第二部分　汉字　**Chinese Characters**　86
　　一、汉字知识 Knowledge about Chinese Characters　86
　　　　1. 汉字的笔画（8） Strokes of Chinese characters (8)
　　　　　　乚　𠃍
　　　　2. 汉字的结构（4） Structures of Chinese characters (4)
　　　　　　左右结构 Left-right structure
　　　　　　左中右结构 Left-middle-right structure
　　二、汉字认读与书写 The Recognition and Writing of Chinese Characters　87

第三部分　日常用语　**Daily Expressions**　87
第四部分　单元实训　**Unit Practical Training**　87
　　车辆管理系统应用实训 Practical Training of Vehicle Managemengt System Application　87
第五部分　单元小结　**Unit Summary**　88

第九单元　条码技术　Unit 9　Bar Code Technology　91

第一部分　课文　**Texts**　92
　　一、热身 Warm-up　92
　　二、课文 Texts　94
　　三、视听说 Viewing, Listening and Speaking　95
　　四、学以致用 Practicing What You Have Learnt　96
　　五、小知识 Tips　97

V

第二部分 汉字 **Chinese Characters**	97
一、汉字知识 Knowledge about Chinese Characters	97
1. 汉字的笔画（9） Strokes of Chinese characters (9)	
乛 乚	
2. 汉字的结构（5） Structures of Chinese characters (5)	
全包围结构 Fully-enclosed structure	
半包围结构 Semi-enclosed structure	
二、汉字认读与书写 The Recognition and Writing of Chinese Characters	98
第三部分 日常用语 **Daily Expressions**	98
第四部分 单元实训 **Unit Practical Training**	98
条形码技术应用实训 Practical Training of Bar Code Technology Application	98
第五部分 单元小结 **Unit Summary**	99

第十单元　全球定位系统（GPS）　Unit 10　Global Positioning System (GPS)　101

第一部分 课文 **Texts**	102
一、热身 Warm-up	102
二、课文 Texts	103
三、视听说 Viewing, Listening and Speaking	105
四、学以致用 Practicing What You Have Learnt	106
五、小知识 Tips	107
第二部分 汉字 **Chinese Characters**	108
一、汉字知识 Knowledge about Chinese Characters	108
1. 汉字的笔画（总表） Strokes of Chinese characters (general table)	
2. 汉字的笔顺（总表） Stroke orders of Chinese characters (general table)	
3. 汉字的结构（总表） Structures of Chinese characters (general table)	
二、汉字认读与书写 The Recognition and Writing of Chinese Characters	109
第三部分 日常用语 **Daily Expressions**	109
第四部分 单元实训 **Unit Practical Training**	109
GPS 应用实训 Practical Training of GPS Application	109
第五部分 单元小结 **Unit Summary**	110

附录　Appendixes　113

词语总表 **Vocabulary**	113
视频脚本 **Video Scripts**	122
参考答案 **Reference Answers**	127

1

Dìngdān chǔlǐ
订单处理
Order Processing

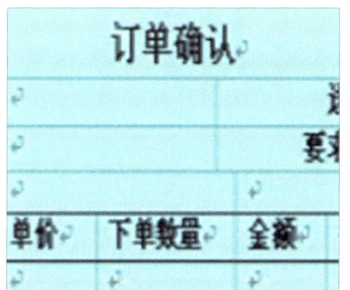

dìngdān quèrèn
订单 确认
confirm the order

jiànlì kèhù dàng'àn
建立客户档案
create the customer file

jiēshòu dìnghuò
接受 订货
take an order

shèdìng dìngdānhào
设定 订单号
set an order number

cúnhuò fēnpèi
存货 分配
allocate the inventory

1

题解 Introduction

1. 学习内容：订单处理的流程和具体内容。
   Learning content: The process and specific content of order processing.
2. 知识目标：掌握与订单处理相关的核心词语及表达，学习汉字的笔画"一""丨""丿""㇏"和笔顺"先横后竖、先撇后捺"，学写相关汉字。
   Knowledge objectives: Grasp the core vocabulary and expressions related to order processing, learn the strokes "一", "丨", "丿", "㇏" and stroke order "horizontal strokes before vertical strokes, left-falling strokes before right-falling strokes" of Chinese characters, and learn to write the related Chinese characters.
3. 技能目标：能在物流管理中完成订单处理任务。
   Skill objective: Be able to complete order processing in logistics management.

第一部分　Part 1

课文　Texts

一、热身　rèshēn　Warm-up

1. 给词语选择对应的图片。Choose the corresponding pictures for the words.

A.

B.

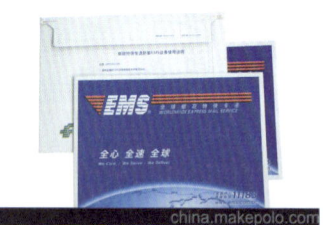

C.

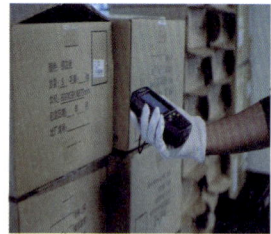

D.

❶ chuánzhēn dìnghuò
   传真 订货 ＿＿＿＿
   order by fax

❷ huòjià biāoqiān pèihé shǒuchí zhōngduān dìnghuò
   货架 标签 配合 手持 终端 订货 ＿＿＿＿
   order by shelf labels with a handheld terminal

❸ kǒutóu dìnghuò
   口头 订货 ＿＿＿＿
   verbal order

❹ yóujì dìnghuò
   邮寄 订货 ＿＿＿＿
   order by mail

2. 观看介绍订单处理步骤的视频，将下列选项按订单处理步骤的先后顺序排序。**Watch the video introducing the steps of order processing and arrange the following options according to order processing steps.**

A. jiànlì kèhù dàng'àn
建立 客户 档案
create the customer file

B. shèdìng dìngdānhào
设定 订单号
set the order number

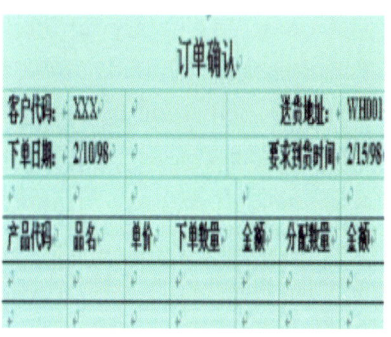

C. dìngdān quèrèn
订单 确认
confirm the order

D. cúnhuò fēnpèi
存货 分配
allocate the inventory

E. jiēshòu dìnghuò
接受 订货
take an order

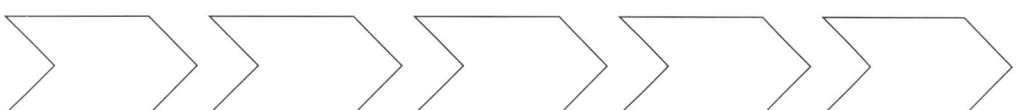

二、课文 kèwén Texts

A 🎧 01-01

Dìngdān shì qǐyè cǎigòu bùmén xiàng gōngyìngshāng fāchū de dìnghuò píngjù, tā dàibiǎo
订单是企业采购部门向供应商发出的订货凭据，它代表
kèhù de xūqiú. Dìngdān yìbān bāohán kèhù xìnxī、yùnshū xìnxī、jiésuàn fāngshì、shāngpǐn
客户的需求。订单一般包含客户信息、运输信息、结算方式、商品
míngchēng、shāngpǐn xínghào、dìnggòu shùliàng、shāngpǐn dānjià děng xìnxī.
名称、商品型号、订购数量、商品单价等信息。

译文 yìwén Text in English

An order is an order certificate issued by the purchasing department of the enterprise to the supplier, which represents the needs of the customer. An order usually contains customer information, transportation information, settlement method, commodity name, commodity model, order quantity, the unit price of the commodity, etc.

普通词语 pǔtōng cíyǔ General Vocabulary 🎧 01-02

1.	向	xiàng	prep.	indicating target of action
2.	发出	fāchū	v.	issued by
3.	它	tā	pron.	it
4.	代表	dàibiǎo	v.	represent, stand for
5.	需求	xūqiú	n.	need
6.	一般	yìbān	adj.	usual
7.	包含	bāohán	v.	contain

专业词语 zhuānyè cíyǔ Specialized Vocabulary 🎧 01-03

1.	企业	qǐyè	n.	enterprise
2.	采购	cǎigòu	v.	purchase
3.	部门	bùmén	n.	department
4.	供应商	gōngyìngshāng	n.	supplier
5.	订货	dìng//huò	v.	order goods
6.	凭据	píngjù	n.	evidence, proof
7.	结算方式	jiésuàn fāngshì	phr.	settlement method
8.	商品	shāngpǐn	n.	commodity
9.	型号	xínghào	n.	model

| 10. | 订购 | dìnggòu | v. | order |
| 11. | 单价 | dānjià | n. | unit price |

B 🎧 01-04

订单处理是从接到客户订单到着手准备拣货之间的作业阶段，涉及客户订单资料确认、存货查询和单据处理等流程。订单处理要求做到迅速、准确、服务周到。

译文 yìwén Text in English

Order processing is the stage of operation from receiving a customer's order to setting out to make preparations for picking up the goods. It involves processes such as customer order file confirmation, inventory inquiry and receipt processing. Order processing requires to be prompt, accurate, and considerate in service.

普通词语 pǔtōng cíyǔ General Vocabulary 🎧 01-05

1.	处理	chǔlǐ	v.	handle, deal with
2.	从	cóng	prep.	from
3.	接到	jiēdào	phr.	receive
	到	dào	v.	used as a complement of a verb indicating the result of an action
4.	到	dào	v.	up until/to, by
5.	着手	zhuóshǒu	v.	put one's hand to
6.	之间	zhījiān	n.	space between/among things/people
7.	阶段	jiēduàn	n.	stage, phase
8.	涉及	shèjí	v.	involve
9.	要求	yāoqiú	v.	require
10.	迅速	xùnsù	adj.	prompt
11.	准确	zhǔnquè	adj.	accurate
12.	服务	fúwù	n.	service

专业词语 zhuānyè cíyǔ Specialized Vocabulary 🎧 01-06

| 1. | 资料 | zīliào | n. | data, information |
| 2. | 确认 | quèrèn | v. | confirm |

3.	存货	cúnhuò	n.	inventory
4.	查询	cháxún	v.	inquiry
5.	单据	dānjù	n.	receipt, voucher
6.	周到	zhōudào	adj.	considerate

三、视听说　shì-tīng-shuō　Viewing, Listening and Speaking

观看介绍电子订货方式的视频，说一说电子订货方式有哪些优势。Watch the video introducing electronic ordering, and talk about the advantages of electronic ordering.

diànzǐ dìnghuò fāngshì
电子订货方式
electronic ordering

　　chuánsòng sùdù màn　　　kěkàoxìng gāo　　　　zhǔnquèxìng gāo　　　　fúwù shuǐpíng dī
A. 传送 速度 慢　　B. 可靠性 高　　C. 准确性 高　　D. 服务 水平 低

　　zhǔnquèxìng dī　　　　chuánsòng sùdù kuài　　　kěkàoxìng dī　　　　fúwù shuǐpíng gāo
E. 准确性 低　　F. 传送 速度 快　　G. 可靠性 低　　H. 服务 水平 高

diànzǐ dìnghuò fāngshì de yōushì
电子 订货 方式 的 优势：_____

the advantages of electronic ordering

四、学以致用　xuéyǐzhìyòng　Practicing What You Have Learnt

观看介绍订单录入过程的视频，并根据下列订单提供的信息完成连线。Watch the video introducing order entry process, and complete the match of columns based on the information provided by the following order.

dìngdān lùrù guòchéng
订单录入过程
order entry process

订单处理 1
Order Processing

拣货单编号：JHD0001				客户订单编号：DD008					
客户名称：南京市天马有限公司				出货日期：2023 年 6 月 9 日					
拣货人：李明				拣货日期：2023 年 6 月 9 日					
核查人：张亮				核查时间：2023 年 6 月 9 日					
序号	储位号码	货物名称	规格型号	货物编号	包装单位			数量	备注
					整托盘	箱	单件		
1	A010102	白糖	500 克 / 袋	060804			√	6 袋	
2	B020301	牙刷	80 支 / 箱	030412		√		1 箱	
3	C060403	牛奶	24 盒 / 箱	090248	√			1 箱	

❶ 客户订单编号
kèhù dìngdān biānhào
customer order No.

A. B020301

❷ 出货日期
chūhuò rìqī
date of dispatch

B. 6 袋

❸ 牙刷的储位号码
yáshuā de chǔwèi hàomǎ
storage location No. of toothbrushes

C. DD008

❹ 牛奶的规格型号
niúnǎi de guīgé xínghào
specifications and models of milk

D. 24 盒 / 箱

❺ 白糖的数量
báitáng de shùliàng
quantity of sugar

E. 2023 年 6 月 9 日

7

五、小知识　xiǎo zhīshi　Tips

订单处理如何让客户产生信赖感
Dìngdān chǔlǐ rúhé ràng kèhù chǎnshēng xìnlàigǎn

订单处理是客户服务的开端，也是服务质量得以保障的根本。在订单处理过程中，要使客户产生信赖感，就要做到尽量缩短订货周期，提供紧急订货，减少缺货情况，不忽略小批量订货的客户，以及随时提供订单处理服务。

Dìngdān chǔlǐ shì kèhù fúwù de kāiduān, yě shì fúwù zhìliàng déyǐ bǎozhàng de gēnběn. Zài dìngdān chǔlǐ guòchéng zhōng, yào shǐ kèhù chǎnshēng xìnlàigǎn, jiù yào zuòdào jǐnliàng suōduǎn dìnghuò zhōuqī, tígōng jǐnjí dìnghuò, jiǎnshǎo quē huò qíngkuàng, bù hūluè xiǎo pīliàng dìnghuò de kèhù, yǐjí suíshí tígōng dìngdān chǔlǐ fúwù.

How to Win the Customer's Trust Through Order Processing

Order processing is the beginning of customer service, as well as the basis for ensuring service quality. During order processing process, in order to create a sense of trust among customers, ordering cycle shall be shortened as much as possible, rush orders shall be provided, stockouts shall be reduced, customers who order small batches shall not be ignored, and order processing shall be provided at any time.

第二部分　Part 2
汉字　Chinese Characters

一、汉字知识　Hànzì zhīshi　Knowledge about Chinese Characters

1. 汉字的笔画（1）Strokes of Chinese characters (1)

笔画 Strokes	名称 Names	例字 Examples
一	横 héng	二
丨	竖 shù	十
丿	撇 piě	人
丶	捺 nà	八

2. 汉字的笔顺（1）Stroke orders of Chinese characters (1)

规则 Rules	例字 Examples	笔顺 Stroke orders
先横后竖 Horizontal strokes before vertical strokes	十	一 十
先撇后捺 Left-falling strokes before right-falling strokes	人　八	丿 人　丿 八

8

二、汉字认读与书写　Hànzì rèndú yǔ shūxiě　The Recognition and Writing of Chinese Characters

认读下列词语，并试着读写构成词语的汉字。Recognize the following words, and try to read and write the Chinese characters forming these words.

结算　　方式　　存货　　查询　　单据　　处理

结			算			方			式		
存			货			查			询		
单			据			处			理		

第三部分　Part 3　日常用语 Daily Expressions

❶ 劳驾，帮我叫辆出租车。Láojià, bāng wǒ jiào liàng chūzūchē. Excuse me, please get me a taxi.
❷ 明天见。Míngtiān jiàn. See you tomorrow.
❸ 不见不散。Bújiàn-búsàn. Be there or be square.

第四部分　Part 4　单元实训 Unit Practical Training

订单处理实训　dìngdān chǔlǐ shíxùn　Practical Training of Order Processing

实训目的 Training purpose
通过本次实训，掌握订单处理的主要步骤，并能完成订单处理作业。
Through this practical training, master the main steps of order processing, and be able to complete order processing operations.

实训组织 Training organization
每组 5 人，设定一名组长。
Each group consists of 5 trainees, with a group leader.

实训步骤 Training steps
❶ 将参加实训的人员分成若干小组，每组 5 人；
Divide the trainees into groups of 5;
❷ 第一个人完成接受订货作业；
The first trainee completes the operation of accepting an order;
❸ 第二个人完成订单确认作业；
The second one completes the operation of confirming the order;

❹ 第三个人完成设定订单号作业；

The third one completes the operation of setting the order number;

❺ 第四个人完成建立客户档案作业；

The fourth one completes the operation of creating the customer file;

❻ 第五个人完成存货分配作业。

The fifth one completes the operation of allocating the inventory.

❼ 五个人轮流完成五项作业。

These five trainees take turns to complete the five operations.

❽ 教师总结评价，实训结束。

The teacher summarizes and evaluates, and the training ends.

第五部分　Part 5　单元小结 Unit Summary

cíyǔ 词语 Vocabulary

普通词语　General Vocabulary

1.	向	xiàng	prep.	*indicating target of action*
2.	发出	fāchū	v.	issued by
3.	它	tā	pron.	it
4.	代表	dàibiǎo	v.	represent, stand for
5.	需求	xūqiú	n.	need
6.	一般	yìbān	adj.	usual
7.	包含	bāohán	v.	contain
8.	处理	chǔlǐ	v.	handle, deal with
9.	从	cóng	prep.	from
10.	接到	jiēdào	phr.	receive
	到	dào	v.	*used as a complement of a verb indicating the result of an action*
11.	到	dào	v.	up until/to, by
12.	着手	zhuóshǒu	v.	put one's hand to
13.	之间	zhījiān	n.	space between/among things/people
14.	阶段	jiēduàn	n.	stage, phase
15.	涉及	shèjí	v.	involve
16.	要求	yāoqiú	v.	require
17.	迅速	xùnsù	adj.	prompt
18.	准确	zhǔnquè	adj.	accurate
19.	服务	fúwù	n.	service

订单处理 1
Order Processing

词语 Vocabulary

专业词语　Specialized Vocabulary

1.	企业	qǐyè	n.	enterprise
2.	采购	cǎigòu	v.	purchase
3.	部门	bùmén	n.	department
4.	供应商	gōngyìngshāng	n.	supplier
5.	订货	dìng//huò	v.	order goods
6.	凭据	píngjù	n.	evidence, proof
7.	结算方式	jiésuàn fāngshì	phr.	settlement method
8.	商品	shāngpǐn	n.	commodity
9.	型号	xínghào	n.	model
10.	订购	dìnggòu	v.	order
11.	单价	dānjià	n.	unit price
12.	资料	zīliào	n.	data, information
13.	确认	quèrèn	v.	confirm
14.	存货	cúnhuò	n.	inventory
15.	查询	cháxún	v.	inquiry
16.	单据	dānjù	n.	receipt, voucher
17.	周到	zhōudào	adj.	considerate

补充专业词语　Supplementary Specialized Vocabulary

1.	客户档案	kèhù dàng'àn	phr.	customer file
2.	设定订单号	shèdìng dìngdānhào	phr.	set an order number
3.	存货分配	cúnhuò fēnpèi	phr.	allocate the inventory
4.	订货周期	dìnghuò zhōuqī	phr.	ordering cycle
5.	电子订货	diànzǐ dìnghuò	phr.	electronic ordering

句子 Sentences

1. 订单一般包含客户信息、运输信息、结算方式、商品名称、商品型号、订购数量、商品单价等信息。
2. 订单处理涉及客户订单资料确认、存货查询和单据处理等流程。
3. 订单处理的过程主要包括接受订货、订单确认、设定订单号、建立客户档案、存货分配等步骤。
4. 电子订货方式具有传送速度快，可靠性、准确性高，客户服务水平高等优点。

11

2 Liútōng jiāgōng
流通加工
Distribution Processing

shēngchǎn jiāgōng 生产 加工 production processing	VS	liútōng jiāgōng 流通加工 distribution processing
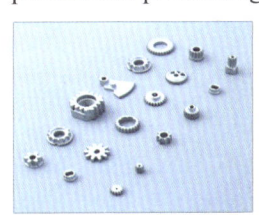 yuáncáiliào、língpèijiàn、bànchéngpǐn 原材料、零配件、半成品 raw materials, spare parts, and semi-finished products	jiāgōng duìxiàng bù tóng 加工 对象 不同 the processing objects are different	 shāngpǐn 商品 commodities
 shēngchǎn qǐyè 生产 企业 a production enterprise	zǔzhīzhě bù tóng 组织者不同 the organizers are different	 shāngyè qǐyè huò wùliú qǐyè 商业 企业或物流 企业 a commercial enterprise or logistics enterprise
 fùzá, jìshù yāoqiú gāo 复杂，技术要求高 complex, with high technical requirements	jiāgōng chéngdù bù tóng 加工 程度 不同 the degrees of processing are different	 jiǎndān 简单 simple
 chuàngzào jiàzhí hé shǐyòng jiàzhí 创造 价值和使用 价值 to create value and use value	jiāgōng mùdì bù tóng 加工目的不同 the purposes of processing are different	 wánshàn hé tígāo shāngpǐn de shǐyòng jiàzhí 完善和提高 商品 的使用 价值 to perfect and improve the use value of commodities

13

题解 Introduction

1. 学习内容：流通加工、生产加工的概念和区别以及流通加工的种类。
   Learning content: The definition of distribution processing and production processing, the difference between them and the types of distribution processing.
2. 知识目标：掌握与流通加工相关的核心词语及表达，学习汉字的笔画 "、" "㇇" "㇄" "㇟" 和笔顺 "先上后下、先左后右"，学写相关汉字。
   Knowledge objectives: Grasp the core vocabulary and expressions related to distribution processing, learn the strokes "、", "㇇", "㇄", "㇟" and stroke order "upper strokes before lower strokes, left-side strokes before right-side strokes" of Chinese characters, and learn to write the related Chinese characters.
3. 技能目标：掌握不同种类的流通加工在生活中的实际运用。
   Skill objective: Master the practical application of the different types of distribution processing in life.

第一部分 Part 1

课文 Texts

一、热身 rèshēn Warm-up

1. 给词语选择对应的图片。Choose the corresponding pictures for the words.

A.

B.

C.

D.

① lěngdòng jiāgōng
冷冻 加工 _____
freezing processing

② jīngzhì jiāgōng
精制 加工 _____
refining processing

③ mùcái liútōng jiāgōng
木材 流通 加工 _____
wood distribution processing

④ miánhuā liútōng jiāgōng
棉花 流通 加工 _____
cotton distribution processing

2. 看视频，了解生产加工和流通加工的区别，说一说它们分别有哪些特征并连线。**Watch the video to learn about the differences between production processing and distribution processing, talk about their respective characteristics and match the two columns.**

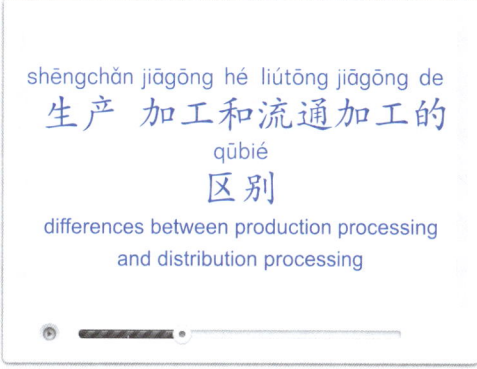

A. jiāgōng shāngpǐn
加工 商品
processing commodities

B. jiāgōng yuáncáiliào
加工 原材料
processing raw materials

C. zǔzhīzhě shì wùliú qǐyè
组织者是物流企业
organizer being a logistics enterprise

❶ shēngchǎn jiāgōng
生产 加工
production processing

D. zǔzhīzhě shì shēngchǎn qǐyè
组织者是 生产 企业
organizer being a production enterprise

❷ liútōng jiāgōng
流通加工
distribution processing

E. fùzá jiāgōng
复杂加工
complex processing

F. jiǎndān jiāgōng
简单加工
simple processing

G. chuàngzào jiàzhí
创造 价值
creating value

H. tíshēng shǐyòng jiàzhí
提升 使用价值
improving use value

二、课文　kèwén　Texts

A 02-01

Liútōng jiāgōng shì duì zuìzhōng shāngpǐn jìnxíng de bāozhuāng、fēngē、jìliàng、fēnjiǎn、
流通加工是对最终商品进行的包装、分割、计量、分拣、

tiē biāozhì、shuān biāoqiān、zǔzhuāng děng jiǎndān zài jiāgōng，shì duì fùzá shēngchǎn jiāgōng de
贴标志、拴标签、组装等简单再加工，是对复杂生产加工的

fǔzhù hé bǔchōng.
辅助和补充。

译文 yìwén Text in English

Distribution processing is the simple reprocessing of final commodities, such as packaging, division, metering, sorting, pasting marks, labeling, assembling, etc., which is auxiliary and complementary to complex production processing.

bāozhuāng
包装
packaging

fēngē
分割
division

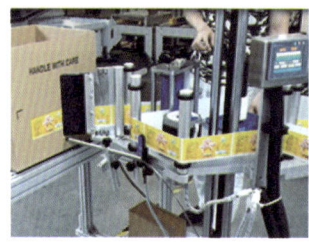

shuān biāoqiān
拴标签
labeling

tiē biāozhì
贴标志
pasting marks

zǔzhuāng
组装
assembling

流通加工
Distribution Processing

普通词语 pǔtōng cíyǔ General Vocabulary 🎧 02-02

1.	对	duì	prep.	concerning, regarding
2.	进行	jìnxíng	v.	carry out
3.	简单	jiǎndān	adj.	simple
4.	复杂	fùzá	adj.	complex
5.	辅助	fǔzhù	v.	assist
6.	补充	bǔchōng	v.	replenish, supplement

专业词语 zhuānyè cíyǔ Specialized Vocabulary 🎧 02-03

1.	流通加工	liútōng jiāgōng	phr.	distribution processing
2.	最终商品	zuìzhōng shāngpǐn	phr.	final commodity, final product
3.	分割	fēngē	v.	cut apart, separate
4.	计量	jìliàng	v.	measure
5.	分拣	fēnjiǎn	v.	sort
6.	贴标志	tiē biāozhì	phr.	paste marks
7.	拴标签	shuān biāoqiān	phr.	label
	标签	biāoqiān	n.	label
8.	组装	zǔzhuāng	v.	assemble
9.	再加工	zài jiāgōng	phr.	reprocess
10.	生产加工	shēngchǎn jiāgōng	phr.	production processing

B 🎧 02-04

Shēngxiān shípǐn de liútōng jiāgōng zhǔyào yǒu lěngdòng jiāgōng、fēn xuǎn jiāgōng、jīngzhì jiāgōng hé fēn zhuāng jiāgōng. Xīnxiān shūcài jīngguò liútōng jiāgōng hòu chéngwéi kěyǐ zhíjiē pēngtiáo shíyòng de jìngcài.

生鲜食品的流通加工主要有冷冻加工、分选加工、精制加工和分装加工。新鲜蔬菜经过流通加工后成为可以直接烹调食用的净菜。

中文＋物流管理（中级）

译文 yìwén Text in English

The distribution processing of fresh food mainly includes freezing processing, sorting processing, refining processing and packaging processing. Fresh vegetables become clean vegetables that can be cooked and eaten directly after the distribution processing.

lěngdòng jiāgōng
冷冻 加工
freezing processing

fēn xuǎn jiāgōng
分 选 加工
sorting processing

jīngzhì jiāgōng
精制 加工
refining processing

fēn zhuāng jiāgōng
分 装 加工
packaging processing

普通词语 pǔtōng cíyǔ General Vocabulary 02-05

1.	生鲜	shēngxiān	n.	raw and fresh
2.	食品	shípǐn	n.	food
3.	主要	zhǔyào	adj.	main
4.	新鲜	xīnxiān	adj.	fresh
5.	蔬菜	shūcài	n.	vegetable
6.	经过	jīngguò	v.	(of action, etc.) go through
7.	后	hòu	n.	(of time) (in) future
8.	成为	chéngwéi	v.	become
9.	直接	zhíjiē	adj.	direct
10.	烹调	pēngtiáo	v.	cook
11.	食用	shíyòng	v.	eat
12.	净菜	jìngcài	n.	clean vegetable

流通加工 2
Distribution Processing

专业词语 zhuānyè cíyǔ Specialized Vocabulary 🎧 02-06

1.	冷冻加工	lěngdòng jiāgōng	phr.	freezing processing
2.	分选加工	fēn xuǎn jiāgōng	phr.	sorting processing
3.	精制加工	jīngzhì jiāgōng	phr.	refining processing
4.	分装加工	fēn zhuāng jiāgōng	phr.	packaging processing

三、视听说 shì-tīng-shuō Viewing, Listening and Speaking

看视频，了解什么是生产加工和流通加工，并判断下列活动属于生产加工还是流通加工。**Watch the video to understand what production processing and distribution processing are, and determine whether the following activities fall under production processing or distribution processing.**

shēngchǎn jiāgōng hé liútōng jiāgōng de
生产 加工和流通加工的
nèihán
内涵
connotation of production processing and distribution processing

A.
zìxíngchē zhuānmàidiàn zǔzhuāng
自行车 专卖店 组装
zìxíngchē
自行车
assembling bicycles by bicycle stores

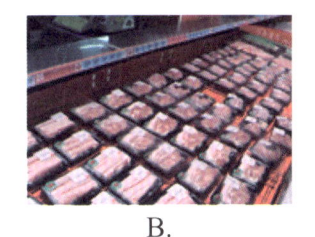

B.
chāoshì fēngē zhūròu
超市 分割 猪肉
cutting pork in supermarkets

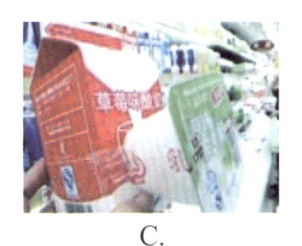

C.
chāoshì zhōng de shāngpǐn kǔnzài yìqǐ
超市 中 的 商品 捆在一起
dāpèi xiāoshòu
搭配 销售
bundling goods together for tie-in sale in supermarkets

D.
shēngchǎn sīchóu chènshān
生产 丝绸 衬衫
producing silk shirts

E.
shēngchǎn huǒtuǐcháng
生产 火腿肠
producing ham sausages

19

四、学以致用 xuéyǐzhìyòng Practicing What You Have Learnt

看视频，了解生鲜产品的四种流通加工方式，并为下列产品选择合适的流通加工方式。Watch the video to understand the four methods of distribution processing of fresh products and choose the appropriate distribution processing method for the following products.

shēngxiān chǎnpǐn de liútōng jiāgōng
生鲜 产品的流通加工
fāngshì
方式
methods of distribution processing of fresh products

A.
yú、 xiā dīwēn lěngdòng
鱼、虾低温 冷冻
low temperature freezing of fish and shrimp

B.
míhóutáo àn dàxiǎo
猕猴桃按大小
tiāoxuǎn fēnlèi
挑选 分类
picking and sorting of kiwifruits by size

C.
shūcài xǐjìng fēn zhuāng
蔬菜洗净分 装
cleaning and packaging of vegetables

D.
huāshēngmǐ yóu sǎnzhuāng
花生米 由 散装
gǎiwéi xiǎo bāozhuāng
改为小 包装
bulk to small packaging for peanuts

lěngdòng jiāgōng
❶ 冷冻 加工 _____
freezing processing

fēn zhuāng jiāgōng
❷ 分 装 加工 _____
packaging processing

jīngzhì jiāgōng
❸ 精制 加工 _____
refining processing

fēnxuǎn jiāgōng
❹ 分选 加工 _____
sorting processing

五、小知识　xiǎo zhīshi　Tips

Jìngcài
净菜

Jìngcài shì zhǐ xīnxiān shūcài jīngguò fēn jí、 zhěnglǐ、 tiāoxuǎn、 qīngxǐ、 qiēfēn、 bǎoxiān
净菜是指新鲜蔬菜经过 分级、整理、挑选、清洗、切分、保鲜

hé bāozhuāng děng yíxìliè chǔlǐ hòu bǎochí shēngxiān zhuàngtài de zhìpǐn。 Jìngcài xīnxiān gānjìng,
和 包装 等一系列处理后保持 生鲜 状态 的制品。净菜新鲜干净，

shíyòng biànjié, xiāofèizhě gòumǎi hòu bù xūyào zài zuò jìnyíbù chǔlǐ jiù kěyǐ zhíjiē pēngtiáo
食用便捷，消费者 购买后不需要再做进一步处理就可以直接 烹调

chéng cài.
成 菜。

Clean Vegetables

Clean vegetables are the products that are kept fresh after a series of processing such as grading, sorting, picking, washing, cutting, preserving and packaging of fresh vegetables. They are fresh, clean, and convenient to eat. Consumers can cook them directly, requiring no further processing after purchasing.

第二部分　Part 2
汉字　Chinese Characters

一、汉字知识　Hànzì zhīshi　Knowledge about Chinese Characters

1. 汉字的笔画（2）Strokes of Chinese characters (2)

笔画 Strokes	名称 Names	例字 Examples
丶	点 diǎn	六
ㄱ	横折 héngzhé	口、日、五
ㄴ	竖折 shùzhé	山
ㄥ	撇折 piězhé	么

2. 汉字的笔顺（2）Stroke orders of Chinese characters (2)

规则 Rules	例字 Examples	笔顺 Stroke orders
先上后下 Upper strokes before lower strokes	三	一 二 三
先左后右 Left-side strokes before right-side strokes	人	丿 人

二、汉字认读与书写　Hànzì rèndú yǔ shūxiě　The Recognition and Writing of Chinese Characters

认读下列词语，并试着读写构成词语的汉字。Recognize the following words, and try to read and write the Chinese characters forming these words.

流通加工　　生鲜　　烹调　　辅助　　主要

流			通			加			工		
生			鲜			烹			调		
辅			助			主			要		

第三部分　Part 3
日常用语　Daily Expressions

❶ 你是学生吗？　Nǐ shì xuéshēng ma? Are you a student?

❷ 你爸爸做什么工作？　Nǐ bàba zuò shénme gōngzuò? What does your father do?

第四部分　Part 4
单元实训　Unit Practical Training

流通加工应用实训　liútōng jiāgōng yìngyòng shíxùn
Practical Training of Distribution Processing Application

实训目的 Training purpose

通过本次实训，了解流通加工的作用，能够根据消费者需求对农产品进行分装加工。

Through this practical training, understand the role of distribution processing and be able to carry out the packaging processing of agricultural products according to consumers' demand.

实训组织 Training organization

每组 3 人。

Each group consists of 3 trainees.

实训步骤 Training steps

❶ 准备黄豆（或者其他的农产品）约 20kg；

Prepare about 20kg of soybeans (or other agricultural products);

❷ 将参加实训的人员分成若干小组，每组 3 人；

Divide the trainees into groups of 3;

❸ 第一个人调研消费者（可以由其他组的组员扮演）的单次购买量；

The first trainee surveys the single purchase volume of consumers (can be played by trainees of other groups);

❹ 第二个人根据调研的结果将不同重量的黄豆分装到袋子中；

The second trainee packages soybeans of different weights into bags according to the result of the survey.

❺ 第三个人打印商品的标签，粘贴到袋子上，并完成封口；

The third trainee prints merchandise labels, affixes them to the bags, and seals the bags;

❻ 三个人轮流完成三项作业。

The three trainees take turns to complete these three operations.

❼ 教师总结评价，实训结束。

The teacher summarizes and evaluates, and the training ends.

第五部分　Part 5　单元小结 Unit Summary

词语 Vocabulary

普通词语　General Vocabulary

1.	对	duì	prep.	concerning, regarding
2.	进行	jìnxíng	v.	carry out
3.	简单	jiǎndān	adj.	simple
4.	复杂	fùzá	adj.	complex
5.	辅助	fǔzhù	v.	assist
6.	补充	bǔchōng	v.	replenish, supplement
7.	生鲜	shēngxiān	n.	raw and fresh
8.	食品	shípǐn	n.	food
9.	主要	zhǔyào	adj.	main
10.	新鲜	xīnxiān	adj.	fresh
11.	蔬菜	shūcài	n.	vegetable
12.	经过	jīngguò	v.	(of action, etc.) go through
13.	后	hòu	n.	(of time) (in) future
14.	成为	chéngwéi	v.	become
15.	直接	zhíjiē	adj.	direct
16.	烹调	pēngtiáo	v.	cook
17.	食用	shíyòng	v.	eat
18.	净菜	jìngcài	n.	clean vegetable

专业词语　Specialized Vocabulary

1.	流通加工	liútōng jiāgōng	phr.	distribution processing
2.	最终商品	zuìzhōng shāngpǐn	phr.	final commodity, final product
3.	分割	fēngē	v.	cut apart, separate
4.	计量	jìliàng	v.	measure
5.	分拣	fēnjiǎn	v.	sort
6.	贴标志	tiē biāozhì	phr.	paste marks
7.	拴标签	shuān biāoqiān	phr.	label
	标签	biāoqiān	n.	label
8.	组装	zǔzhuāng	v.	assemble
9.	再加工	zài jiāgōng	phr.	reprocess
10.	生产加工	shēngchǎn jiāgōng	phr.	production processing
11.	冷冻加工	lěngdòng jiāgōng	phr.	freezing processing
12.	分选加工	fēn xuǎn jiāgōng	phr.	sorting processing
13.	精制加工	jīngzhì jiāgōng	phr.	refining processing
14.	分装加工	fēn zhuāng jiāgōng	phr.	packaging processing

补充专业词语　Supplementary Specialized Vocabulary

1.	生产领域	shēngchǎn lǐngyù	phr.	production field
2.	消费领域	xiāofèi lǐngyù	phr.	consumption field
3.	搭配销售	dāpèi xiāoshòu	phr.	tie-in sale
	搭配	dāpèi	v.	arrange according to given requirements, organize in pairs/groups

句子 Sentences

1. 流通加工是对最终商品进行的包装、分割、计量、分拣、贴标志、拴标签、组装等简单再加工。
2. 生鲜食品的流通加工主要有冷冻加工、分选加工、精制加工和分装加工。
3. 新鲜蔬菜经过流通加工后成为可以直接烹调食用的净菜。

3 摘果式拣选
Zhāiguǒshì jiǎnxuǎn
DPS Picking

zhāiguǒshì jiǎnxuǎn de liúchéng
摘果式 拣选 的 流程
the process of DPS picking

jiǎnhuòyuán jiēshōu jiǎn huò rènwu
拣货员 接收 拣货任务
the picker receives the picking task

zhēnduì měi yí gè kèhù dìngdān jìnxíng jiǎnxuǎn
针对 每一个客户订单 进行 拣选
pick goods for each customer's order

jiǎnhuòyuán xúnhuí yú gègè huòwù chǔwèi
拣货员 巡回于各个货物储位
the picker moves aroud various storage locations

jiāng suǒ xū huòwù yīcì qǔchū,
将 所需货物 依次取出，
zhízhì jiǎnxuǎn wánbì
直至 拣选 完毕
take out the required goods in sequence until the picking is completed

> **题解　Introduction**
>
> 1. 学习内容：摘果式拣选的方法、原理和特点。
>   Learning content: The method, principles and characteristics of DPS picking.
> 2. 知识目标：掌握与摘果式拣选相关的核心词语及表达，学习汉字的笔画"㇏""亅""丿""乚"和笔顺"先中间后两边、先外边后里边"，学写相关汉字。
>   Knowledge objectives: Grasp the core vocabulary and expressions related to DPS picking, learn the strokes "㇏", "亅", "丿", "乚" and stroke order "strokes in the middle before those on the both sides", "outside strokes before inside strokes" of Chinese characters, and learn to write the related Chinese characters.
> 3. 技能目标：能在物流拣选作业中实际运用摘果式拣选。
>   Skill objective: Be able to use DPS picking in logistics picking operation.

第一部分　Part 1

课文　Texts

一、热身　rèshēn　Warm-up

1. 给词语选择对应的图片。Choose the corresponding pictures for the words.

A.

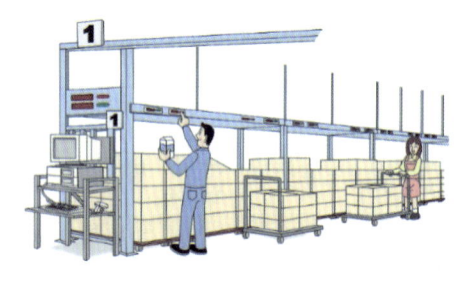

B.

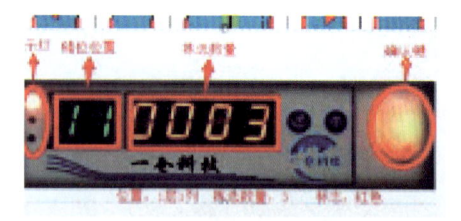

C.

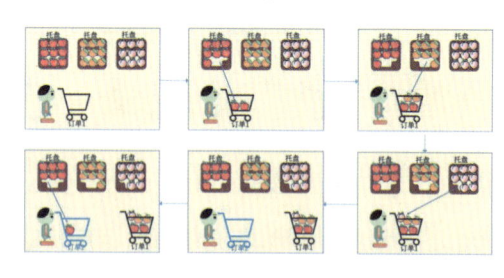

D.

① diànzǐ biāoqiān jiǎnxuǎn xìtǒng
电子 标签 拣选 系统 _____
digital picking system (DPS)

② diànzǐ biāoqiān xiǎnshìqì
电子 标签 显示器 _____
RFID tag display

③ huòwù jiǎnxuǎn
货物 拣选 _____
goods picking

④ zhāiguǒshì jiǎnxuǎn de liúchéng
摘果式 拣选 的 流程 _____
DPS picking process

2. 看视频，了解摘果式拣选的基本流程，并按摘果式拣选流程的顺序给下列选项排序。**Watch the video to understand the basic process of DPS picking, and arrange the following options in order of the DPS picking process.**

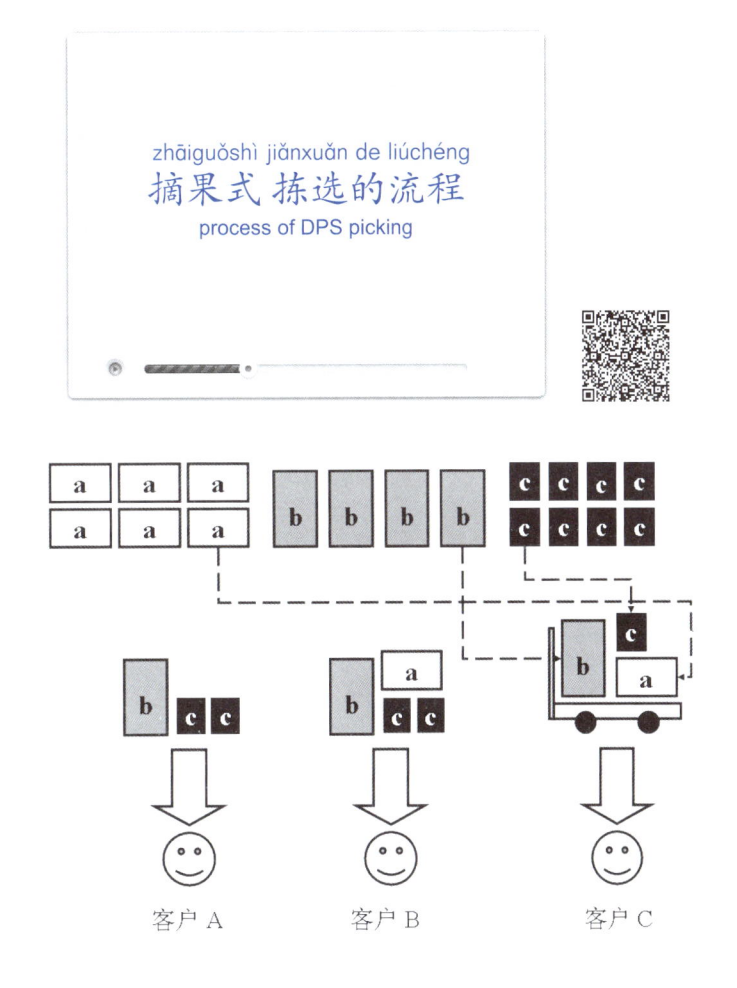

zhāiguǒshì jiǎnxuǎn de liúchéng
摘果式 拣选的流程
process of DPS picking

zhāiguǒshì jiǎnxuǎn shìyìtú
摘果式 拣选示意图
diagram of DPS picking

| jiǎnhuòyuán xúnhuí yú gègè huò-
A. 拣货员 巡回于各个货
wù chǔwèi
物 储位
the picker moves around various storage locations | jiēshōu dào yí gè kèhù dìngdān
B. 接收到一个客户订单
a customer order is received | xiàng zhāi guǒ yíyàng yīcì qǔ-
C. 像 摘果一样依次取
chū huòwù, zhízhì jiǎnxuǎn wánbì
出货物，直至拣选完毕
the picker takes out the goods in sequence, like picking fruit, until the picking is completed |

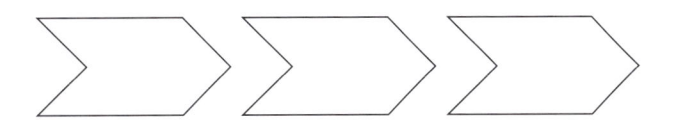

二、课文 kèwén Texts

A 03-01

Zhāiguǒshì jiǎnxuǎn zhēnduì měi yí gè dìngdān jìnxíng jiǎnxuǎn, jiǎnhuò rényuán huò shèbèi
摘果式 拣选 针对每一个订单进行 拣选，拣货 人员 或设备
xúnhuí yú gègè huòwù chǔwèi, jiāng xūyào de huòwù qǔchū, xíngsì zhāi guǒ, měi rén měi cì zhǐ
巡回于各个货物储位，将需要的货物取出，形似摘果，每人每次只
chǔlǐ yí gè kèhù dìngdān.
处理一个客户订单。

译文 yìwén Text in English

DPS picking is the picking process for each order. The picker or picking equipment moves around various storage locations to take out the required goods, like picking fruit. One person handles one customer order at a time.

普通词语 pǔtōng cíyǔ General Vocabulary 03-02

1.	针对	zhēnduì	v.	be aimed at/targeted on/directed against
2.	每	měi	pron.	each
3.	巡回	xúnhuí	v.	tour, go the rounds
4.	于	yú	prep.	(of time/place) in, at, on
5.	各个	gègè	pron.	each, every
	各	gè	pron.	all, every
6.	取	qǔ	v.	get, collect
7.	形似	xíngsì	v.	look like
8.	次	cì	m.	time
9.	只	zhǐ	adv.	only

专业词语 zhuānyè cíyǔ Specialized Vocabulary 03-03

1.	摘果式拣选	zhāiguǒshì jiǎnxuǎn	phr.	DPS picking

28

	摘果	zhāi guǒ	phr.	pick fruit
	拣选	jiǎnxuǎn	v.	pick, select
2.	储位	chǔwèi	n.	storage location

B 🎧 03-04

摘果式拣选简单、易于操作,对单个订单的响应速度快,但行走距离较远,动作较多,耗时较长,所以它适用于货物品种少、订单量大的情况。

译文 yìwén Text in English

DPS picking is simple and easy to operate, and responds quickly to a single order, but it requires longer travel distance, more actions and longer time, so it is suitable for the situation with a small variety of goods and large order quantity.

普通词语 pǔtōng cíyǔ General Vocabulary 🎧 03-05

1.	易于	yìyú	v.	(of sth.) be easy (to do)
2.	操作	cāozuò	v.	operate
3.	单个	dāngè	adj.	single
4.	快	kuài	adj.	quick, fast
5.	但	dàn	conj.	but, yet, still
6.	较	jiào	adv.	comparatively, relatively
7.	远	yuǎn	adj.	(of time/space) far, remote
8.	动作	dòngzuò	n.	action, movement
9.	多	duō	adj.	many, much, more
10.	耗时	hàoshí	v.	consume time
11.	长	cháng	adj.	long

12.	所以	suǒyǐ	conj.	so, therefore
13.	适用	shìyòng	adj.	suitable, applicable
14.	少	shǎo	adj.	few, little
15.	大	dà	adj.	big
16.	情况	qíngkuàng	n.	situation

专业词语 zhuānyè cíyǔ Specialized Vocabulary   🎧 03-06

1.	响应速度	xiǎngyìng sùdù	phr.	response speed
2.	距离	jùlí	n.	distance
3.	品种	pǐnzhǒng	n.	breed, variety
4.	订单量	dìngdānliàng	n.	order quantity

三、视听说 shì-tīng-shuō Viewing, Listening and Speaking

观看介绍电子标签拣选系统的视频，说说下列选项中哪些是电子标签拣选系统的优点。Watch the video introducing the digital picking system, and talk about which of the following options are the advantages of this system.

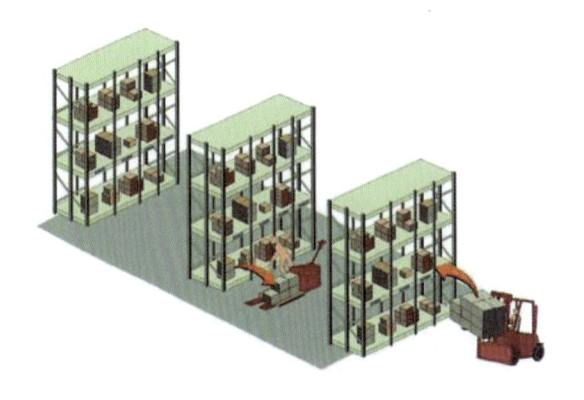

diànzǐ biāoqiān jiǎnxuǎn xìtǒng
电子标签拣选系统
digital picking system

A. 效率高 xiàolǜ gāo — high efficiency
B. 效率低 xiàolǜ dī — low efficiency
C. 差错率高 chācuòlǜ gāo — high error rate
D. 差错率低 chācuòlǜ dī — low error rate

E. 无纸化作业
paperless operation

F. 操作人员上岗快
an operator can take up the post quickly

G. 操作人员上岗慢
it takes time for an operator to take up the post

电子标签拣选系统的优点有：＿＿＿＿＿＿＿＿＿＿＿＿＿＿＿＿＿＿＿＿
the advantages of the digital picking system

四、学以致用 xuéyǐzhìyòng Practicing What You Have Learnt

看视频，了解摘果式拣选的适用条件，并说一说下列哪些订单需要采用摘果式拣选。**Watch the video to understand the applicable conditions for DPS picking, and talk about which of the following orders require adopting DPS picking.**

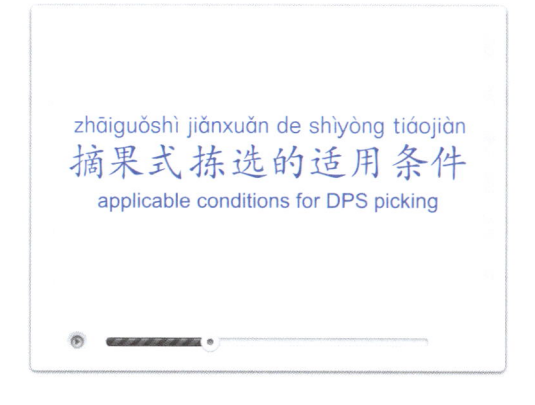

摘果式拣选的适用条件
applicable conditions for DPS picking

A. 订单数量多，但每张订单需要的商品种类有限
there is a large number of orders, but each order has a limited variety of demanded goods

B. 客户的订单需求比较紧急
the need of the customer's order is relatively urgent

C. 不同的订单上，商品种类比较接近
the types of goods on different orders are relatively close to each other

D. 不同客户对商品的需求差异很大
the demand for goods varies greatly from customer to customer

31

五、小知识 xiǎo zhīshi Tips

电子 标签 拣选 系统
diànzǐ biāoqiān jiǎnxuǎn xìtǒng

电子 标签 拣选 系统是一组 安装 在货架储位 上 的电子设备，采用了先进的电子技术和通信技术，通过计算机软件 控制 灯光 信号与数字显示，引导拣货 工人 正确、快速、轻松 地 完成 拣货 工作。

Digital Picking System

The digital picking system is a group of electronic devices installed on the shelf storage locations. Adopting advanced electronic technology and communication technology, with lighting signals and digital display controlled by computer software, it guides pickers to complete the picking work correctly, quickly and easily.

第二部分 Part 2 汉字 Chinese Characters

一、汉字知识 Hànzì zhīshi Knowledge about Chinese Characters

1. 汉字的笔画（3） Strokes of Chinese characters (3)

笔画 Strokes	名称 Names	例字 Examples
㇐	横钩 hénggōu	买
亅	竖钩 shùgōu	小
乚	弯钩 wāngōu	子
㇄	竖弯钩 shùwāngōu	七

2. 汉字的笔顺（3） Stroke orders of Chinese characters (3)

规则 Rules	例字 Examples	笔顺 Stroke orders
先中间后两边 Strokes in the middle before those on both sides	小	亅 小 小
先外边后里边 Outside strokes before inside strokes	问	丶 门 门 问 问

二、汉字认读与书写　Hànzì rèndú yǔ shūxiě　The Recognition and Writing of Chinese Characters

认读下列词语，并试着读写构成词语的汉字。Recognize the following words, and try to read and write the Chinese characters forming these words.

摘果式拣选　　响应　　速度　　耗时　　行走　　距离

摘			果			式			拣		
选			响			应			速		
度			耗			时			行		
走			距			离					

第三部分　Part 3　日常用语 Daily Expressions

① 我来介绍一下儿，这位是李伟先生。Wǒ lái jièshào yíxiàr, zhè wèi shì Lǐ Wěi xiānsheng. Let me introduce you. This is Mr. Li Wei.

② 请问，南京饭店在哪儿？Qǐngwèn, Nánjīng Fàndiàn zài nǎr? Excuse me, where's Nanjing Hotel?

第四部分　Part 4　单元实训 Unit Practical Training

摘果式拣选应用实训　zhāiguǒshì jiǎnxuǎn yìngyòng shíxùn
Practical Training of DPS Picking Application

实训目的 Training purpose

通过本次实训，了解摘果式拣选的原理及应用。

Through this practical training, understand the principles of DPS picking and its applications.

实训组织 Training organization

每组4人，设定1名组长。

Each group consists of 4 trainees, with a group leader.

实训步骤 Training steps

① 教师准备4种不同的货物（如书、本子、笔、水杯等），每种货物的数量不少于8，放置在教室的4个不同位置（模拟仓库储位，有条件的可以在图书馆或者仓库进行）。根据货物数量储备，设计几个订单（注意总订货量不要超过库存量）。

The teacher prepares 4 different kinds of goods (such as books, notebooks, pens, mugs, etc.), with the quantity of each type of goods being no less than 8, and places them in 4 different locations in the classroom (to simulate storage locations, and can be carried out in the library or warehouse if possible). Design several orders based on the quantity of goods in stock (please note that the total order quantity shall not exceed the quantity in stock).

❷ 每组组长组织各个组员随机抽取一个订单。

The leader of each group organizes each group member to draw an order randomly.

❸ 每组组员采用摘果式拣选快速完成拣选任务。

Each group member adopts DPS picking to complete the picking task quickly.

❹ 组长记录各组员的拣选时间和完成情况。

The group leader records the picking time and performance of each group member.

❺ 教师总结评价，实训结束。

The teacher summarizes and evaluates, and the training ends.

第五部分　Part 5　单元小结　Unit Summary

普通词语　General Vocabulary

词语 cíyǔ Vocabulary

1.	针对	zhēnduì	v.	be aimed at / targeted on / directed against
2.	每	měi	pron.	each
3.	巡回	xúnhuí	v.	tour, go the rounds
4.	于	yú	prep.	(of time/place) in, at, on
5.	各个	gègè	pron.	each, every
	各	gè	pron.	all, every
6.	取	qǔ	v.	get, collect
7.	形似	xíngsì	v.	look like
8.	次	cì	m.	time
9.	只	zhǐ	adv.	only
10.	易于	yìyú	v.	(of sth.) be easy (to do)
11.	操作	cāozuò	v.	operate
12.	单个	dāngè	adj.	single
13.	快	kuài	adj.	quick, fast
14.	但	dàn	conj.	but, yet, still
15.	较	jiào	adv.	comparatively, relatively
16.	远	yuǎn	adj.	(of time/space) far, remote

摘果式拣选 3
DPS Picking

词语 Vocabulary

17.	动作	dòngzuò	n.	action, movement
18.	多	duō	adj.	many, much, more
19.	耗时	hàoshí	v.	consume time
20.	长	cháng	adj.	long
21.	所以	suǒyǐ	conj.	so, therefore
22.	适用	shìyòng	adj.	suitable, applicable
23.	少	shǎo	adj.	few, little
24.	大	dà	adj.	big
25.	情况	qíngkuàng	n.	situation

专业词语　Specialized Vocabulary

1.	摘果式拣选	zhāiguǒshì jiǎnxuǎn	phr.	DPS picking
	摘果	zhāi guǒ	phr.	pick fruit
	拣选	jiǎnxuǎn	v.	pick, select
2.	储位	chǔwèi	n.	storage location
3.	响应速度	xiǎngyìng sùdù	phr.	response speed
4.	距离	jùlí	n.	distance
5.	品种	pǐnzhǒng	n.	breed, variety
6.	订单量	dìngdānliàng	n.	order quantity

补充专业词语　Supplementary Specialized Vocabulary

1.	电子标签拣选系统	diànzǐ biāoqiān jiǎnxuǎn xìtǒng	phr.	digital picking system
2.	利弊	lìbì	n.	pros and cons, advantages and disadvantages
3.	波动	bōdòng	v.	fluctuate

句子 Sentences

1. 摘果式拣选针对每一个订单进行拣选，每人每次只处理一个客户订单。
2. 摘果式拣选简单、易于操作，对单个订单的响应速度快，但行走距离较远，动作较多，耗时较长。
3. 摘果式拣选适用于货物品种少、订单量大的情况。

4　播种式拣选
Bōzhǒngshì jiǎnxuǎn
DAS Picking

bōzhǒngshì jiǎnxuǎn de liúchéng
播种式 拣选 的 流程
the process of DAS picking

jiǎnhuòyuán jiēshōu kèhù dìngdān
拣货员 接收客户订单
the picker receives the customer's order

bǎ yídìng shíqī de duō gè kèhù dìngdān huìzǒng chéng yì pī, huìzǒng xiāngtóng pǐnzhǒng de huòwù shùliàng
把一定时期的多个客户订单 汇总 成 一批，汇总 相同 品种的货物 数量
aggregate multiple customers' orders over a certain period of time into a batch, and aggregate the quantity of goods of the same variety

bǎ měi gè pǐnzhǒng de huòwù jiǎnxuǎn chūlái
把每个 品种 的货物 拣选 出来
pick out each variety of goods

zhúgè duì suǒyǒu kèhù jìnxíng fēn huò
逐个对所有客户进行分货
sort the goods for all customers one by one

duì měi gè dìngdān de shāngpǐn jìnxíng fùhé, wánchéng suǒyǒu de pèihuò zuòyè
对每个订单的商品 进行 复核，完成 所有 的配货作业
recheck the goods of each order to complete all the distribution operations of goods

37

题解 Introduction

1. 学习内容：播种式拣选的方法、原理和特点。
   Learning content: The method, principle and characteristics of DAS picking.
2. 知识目标：掌握与播种式拣选相关的核心词语及表达，学习汉字的笔画 "㇒" "㇏" "㇉" "㇟" 和笔顺 "先外后里再封口"，学写相关汉字。
   Knowledge objectives: Grasp the core vocabulary and expressions related to DAS picking, learn the strokes "㇒", "㇏", "㇉", "㇟" and stroke order "outside strokes before inside strokes, and then sealing strokes" of Chinese characters, and learn to write the related Chinese characters.
3. 技能目标：能在物流拣选作业中实际运用播种式拣选。
   Skill objective: Be able to use DAS picking in logistics picking operation.

第一部分 Part 1

课文 Texts

一、热身 rèshēn Warm-up

1. 给词语选择对应的图片。Choose the corresponding pictures for the words.

A.

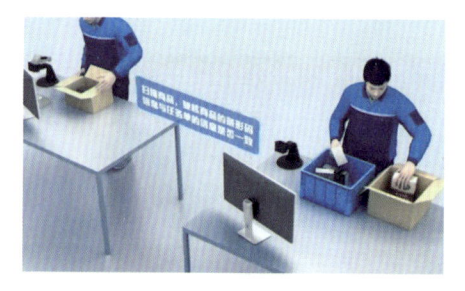

B.

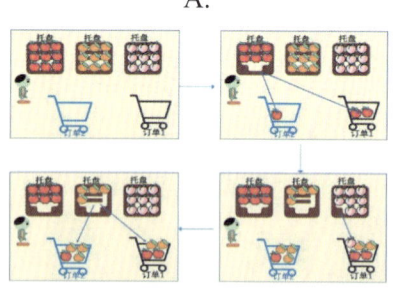

C.

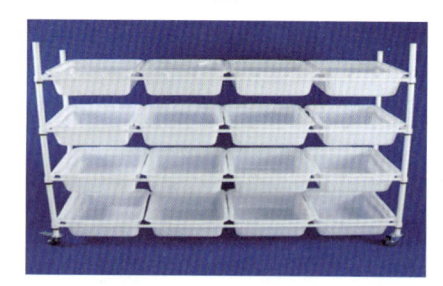

D.

bōzhǒngshì jiǎnxuǎn de liúchéng
❶ 播种式 拣选的流程 _____
DAS picking process

zìdòng fēnjiǎn xìtǒng
❷ 自动分拣系统 _____
automatic sorting system

bōzhǒngshì fēnjiǎnchē
❸ 播种式分拣车 _____
DAS sorting cart

fùhé huánjié
❹ 复核环节 _____
rechecking

38

2. 看视频，了解播种式拣选的基本流程，并按播种式拣选流程的顺序给下列选项排序。**Watch the video to understand the basic process of DAS picking, and arrange the following options in order of the DAS picking process.**

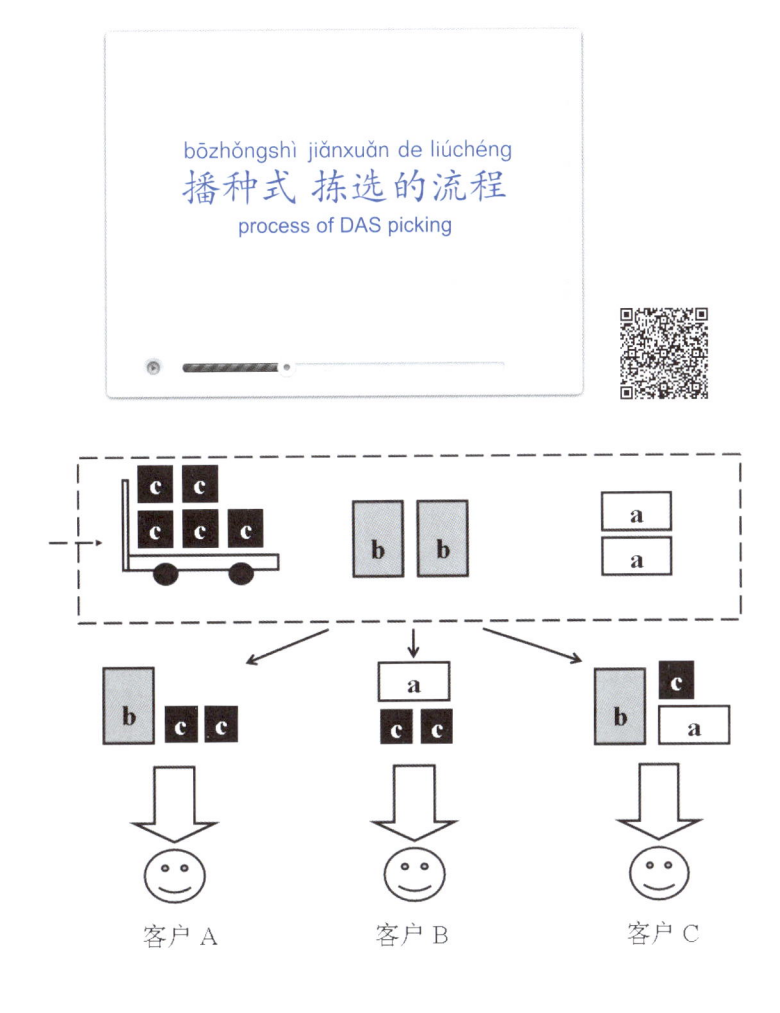

bōzhǒngshì jiǎnxuǎn de liúchéng
播种式 拣选的流程
process of DAS picking

bōzhǒngshì jiǎnxuǎn shìyìtú
播种式 拣选示意图
diagram of DAS picking

| A. jiǎnxuǎn měi gè pǐnzhǒng de huòwù, zhúgè fēn huò gěi suǒyǒu kèhù 拣选 每个 品种 的 货物，逐个分货给所有 客户 pick each variety of goods, and sort them to all customers one by one | B. fùhé měi gè dìngdān de shāngpǐn 复核每个订单的商品 recheck the goods of each order | C. huìzǒng duō gè kèhù dìngdān, bìng huìzǒng xiāngtóng pǐnzhǒng huòwù de shùliàng 汇总多个客户订单，并汇总相同 品种 货物的数量 aggregate multiple customers' orders, and aggregate the quantity of goods of the same variety |

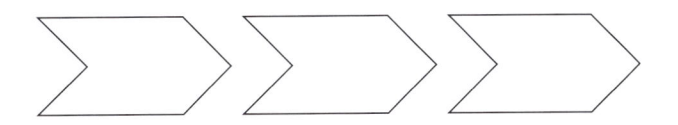

39

二、课文 kèwén Texts

A 04-01

播种式拣选是把多个订单汇总成一批，把相同品种的商品数量进行汇总并一起拣选出来，再逐个品种对所有客户进行分货的拣选方法，形似播种。播种式拣选一次可以拣选多个订单的货物。

译文 yìwén Text in English

DAS (digital assorting system) picking is a picking method that aggregates multiple orders into one batch, aggregates the quantity of goods of the same variety and picks them out together, and then sorts the goods for all customers on a variety-by-variety basis, like seeding. The goods of multiple orders can be picked at one time through DAS picking.

普通词语 pǔtōng cíyǔ General Vocabulary 04-02

1.	成	chéng	v.	amount to (a considerable number/amount)
2.	批	pī	m.	batch
3.	相同	xiāngtóng	adj.	same
4.	并	bìng	conj.	and
5.	一起	yìqǐ	adv.	together
6.	出来	chūlái	v.	used after certain verbs to indicate movement from inside out (towards the speaker)

7.	逐个	zhúgè	adv.	one by one
8.	方法	fāngfǎ	n.	method

专业词语 zhuānyè cíyǔ Specialized Vocabulary 🎧 04-03

1.	播种式拣选	bōzhǒngshì jiǎnxuǎn	phr.	DAS picking
	播种	bō//zhǒng	v.	grow/cultivate by sowing seeds
2.	分货	fēn huò	phr.	sort goods

B 🎧 04-04

Bōzhǒngshì jiǎnxuǎn xiàolǜ gāo, yí cì jiǎnhuòliàng dà, dàn cāozuò fùzá, nándù jiào dà, duì dìngdān de xiǎngyìng sùdù màn, suǒyǐ tā shìyòng yú huòwù pǐnzhǒng hé shùliàng dōu bǐjiào duō、huòwù chónghédù jiào gāo de qíngkuàng.

播种式拣选效率高，一次拣货量大，但操作复杂，难度较大，对订单的响应速度慢，所以它适用于货物品种和数量都比较多、货物重合度较高的情况。

译文 yìwén Text in English

DAS picking is highly efficient because a large quantity of goods can be picked at a time, but its operation is complex and difficult, and its response speed to orders is slow, so it is suitable for the situation where the variety and quantity of goods are relatively large and the overlap ratio of goods is high.

普通词语 pǔtōng cíyǔ General Vocabulary 🎧 04-05

1.	高	gāo	adj.	high
2.	难度	nándù	n.	difficulty
3.	慢	màn	adj.	slow
4.	比较	bǐjiào	adv.	comparatively, relatively

专业词语 zhuānyè cíyǔ Specialized Vocabulary 🎧 04-06

1.	拣货量	jiǎnhuòliàng	n.	picking volume
2.	重合度	chónghédù	n.	overlap ratio

三、视听说 shì-tīng-shuō Viewing, Listening and Speaking

观看介绍自动分拣系统的视频，说说下列哪些是自动分拣系统的优点。Watch the video introducing the automatic sorting system, and talk about which of the followings are the advantages of this system.

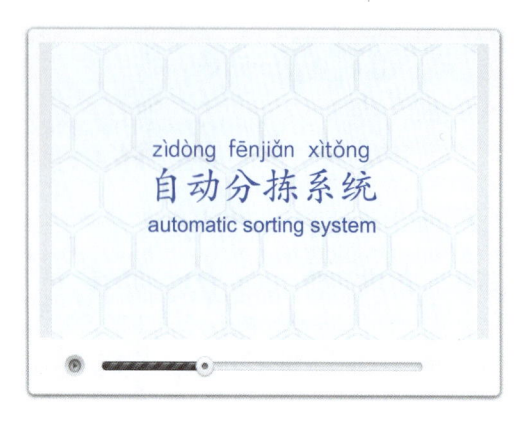

zìdòng fēnjiǎn xìtǒng
自动分拣系统
automatic sorting system

fēnjiǎn xiàolǜ gāo
A. 分拣效率高
high sorting efficiency

fēnjiǎn xiàolǜ dī
B. 分拣效率低
low sorting efficiency

zhǔnquèlǜ gāo
C. 准确率高
high accuracy rate

zhǔnquèlǜ dī
D. 准确率低
low accuracy rate

jiéshěng rénlì
E. 节省人力
saving manpower

jiàngdī huòsǔn
F. 降低货损
reducing cargo damage

shíxiàn shùjù cúnchǔ
G. 实现数据存储
achieving data storage

shíxiàn kě kòng guǎnlǐ
H. 实现可控管理
achieving controllable management

zìdòng fēnjiǎn xìtǒng de yōudiǎn yǒu
自动分拣系统的优点有：_____
the advantages of automatic sorting system

四、学以致用 xuéyǐzhìyòng Practicing What You Have Learnt

看视频，了解播种式拣选的适用条件，说一说下列订单哪些用摘果式拣选、哪些用播种式拣选。Watch the video to understand the applicable conditions for DAS picking, and talk about which of the following orders should use DPS picking and which should use DAS picking.

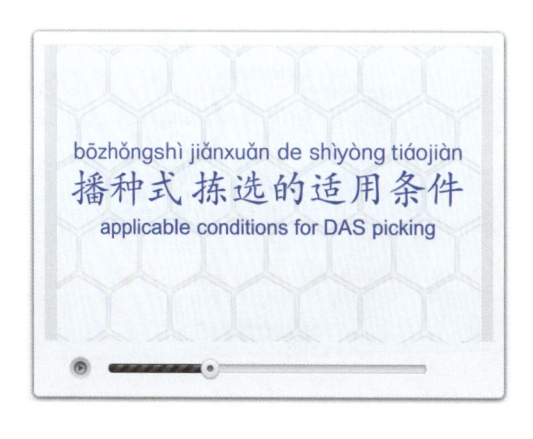

bōzhǒngshì jiǎnxuǎn de shìyòng tiáojiàn
播种式拣选的适用条件
applicable conditions for DAS picking

订单1		订单2		订单3	
货物名称	数量	货物名称	数量	货物名称	数量
《物流管理》	10	《物流管理》	50	《物流管理》	30
《仓储管理》	70	《运输管理》	20	《仓储管理》	40
《配送管理》	20	《配送管理》	30	《配送管理》	30
合计	100	合计	100	合计	100
订单4		订单5		订单6	
货物名称	数量	货物名称	数量	货物名称	数量
《物流管理》	40	《汉语》	15	《配送管理》	40
《运输管理》	60	《英语》	15	《仓储管理》	30
《配送管理》	30	《法语》	15	《运输管理》	40
合计	130	合计	45	合计	110

拣选决策（打"√"）picking decision ("√")			播种式拣选汇总 aggregation of DAS picking	
订单 orders	摘果式拣选 DPS picking	播种式拣选 DAS picking	货物名称 commodity name	数量 quantity
订单1			《物流管理》	
订单2			《仓储管理》	
订单3			《配送管理》	
订单4			《运输管理》	
订单5			《汉语》	
订单6			《英语》	
			《法语》	

五、小知识　xiǎo zhīshi　Tips

自动分拣系统

自动分拣系统能在最短的时间内从庞大的高层货架存储系统中准确找到要出库的商品所在的位置，并按所需数量，从不同

chǔwèi shang qǔchū, zìdòng sòngdào zhǐdìng fēnjiǎnkǒu huò tèdìng qūyù, yǐbiàn zhuāng chē pèisòng.
储位 上 取出，自动 送到 指定 分拣口 或 特定 区域，以便 装 车 配送。

Automatic Picking System

The automatic picking system can find the location of the goods to be outbound delivered in the huge high level shelf storage system accurately in the shortest time, take them out from different storage locations according to the required quantity, and automatically deliver them to the designated sorting ports or specific area for loading and distribution.

第二部分　Part 2　汉字 Chinese Characters

一、汉字知识　Hànzì zhīshi　Knowledge about Chinese Characters

1. 汉字的笔画（4）Strokes of Chinese characters (4)

笔画 Strokes	名称 Names	例字 Examples
㇀	提 tí	习
㇙	竖提 shùtí	衣
㇗	横折提 héngzhétí	语
㇚	撇点 piědiǎn	女

2. 汉字的笔顺（4）Stroke orders of Chinese characters (4)

规则 Rule	例字 Examples	笔顺 Stroke orders
先外后里再封口 Outside strokes before inside strokes, and then sealing strokes	国 日	丨 冂 冂 冋 冈 国 国 国 丨 冂 冃 日

二、汉字认读与书写　Hànzì rèndú yǔ shūxiě　The Recognition and Writing of Chinese Characters

认读下列词语，并试着读写构成词语的汉字。Recognize the following words, and try to read and write the Chinese characters forming these words.

相同　播种　复杂　难度

| 相 | | 同 | | 播 | | 种 | |
| 复 | | 杂 | | 难 | | 度 | |

第三部分　Part 3　日常用语 Daily Expressions

❶ 我们机场见。Wǒmen jīchǎng jiàn. See you at the airport.

❷ 我们电话 / 邮件联系。Wǒmen diànhuà/yóujiàn liánxì. Keep in touch by phone/e-mail.

❸ 下星期一到北京的航班还有票吗？ Xià xīngqīyī dào Běijīng de hángbān hái yǒu piào ma?
Are there any tickets available for next Monday's flight to Beijing?

第四部分　Part 4　单元实训 Unit Practical Training

播种式拣选应用实训　bōzhǒngshì jiǎnxuǎn yìngyòng shíxùn
Practical Training of DAS Picking Application

实训目的 Training purpose

通过本次实训，了解播种式拣选的原理及应用。

Through this practical training, understand the principles of DAS picking and its applications.

实训组织 Training organization

每组 4 人，设定 1 名组长。

Each group consists of 4 trainees, with a group leader.

实训步骤 Training steps

❶ 教师准备 4 种不同的货物（如书、本子、笔、水杯等），每种货物的数量不少于 20，放置在教室的 4 个不同位置（模拟仓库储位，有条件的可以在图书馆或者仓库进行）。根据货物数量储备，设计 8 个订单（注意总订货数量不要超过库存数量）。

The teacher prepares 4 different kinds of goods (such as books, notebooks, pens, mugs, etc.), with the quantity of each type of goods being no less than 20, and places them in 4 different locations in the classroom (to simulate storage locations, and can be carried out in the library or warehouse if possible). Design 8 orders based on the quantity of goods in stock (please note that the total order quantity shall not exceed the quantity in stock).

❷ 每组组长随机抽取 4 个订单，汇总同类商品数量，分派拣选任务。

The leader of each group randomly draws 4 orders, summarizes the quantity of goods of the same variety and assigns the picking task.

❸ 每个组员根据任务要求，采用播种式拣选快速完成拣选任务。

According to the task requirements, each group member adopts DAS picking to complete the picking task quickly.

❹ 组长做最后的复核，并记录任务完成情况。
The group leader makes the final recheck and records the performance of the task.

❺ 组长汇报整组任务完成情况，教师总结评价，实训结束。
The group leader reports the performance of the task of the whole group, the teacher summarizes and evaluates, and the training ends.

第五部分　Part 5　单元小结　Unit Summary

词语 cíyǔ Vocabulary

普通词语　General Vocabulary

1.	成	chéng	v.	amount to (a considerable number/amount)
2.	批	pī	m.	batch
3.	相同	xiāngtóng	adj.	same
4.	并	bìng	conj.	and
5.	一起	yìqǐ	adv.	together
6.	出来	chūlái	v.	used after certain verbs to indicate movement from inside out (towards the speaker)
7.	逐个	zhúgè	adv.	one by one
8.	方法	fāngfǎ	n.	method
9.	高	gāo	adj.	high
10.	难度	nándù	n.	difficulty
11.	慢	màn	adj.	slow
12.	比较	bǐjiào	adv.	comparatively, relatively

专业词语　Specialized Vocabulary

1.	播种式拣选	bōzhǒngshì jiǎnxuǎn	phr.	DAS picking
	播种	bō//zhǒng	v.	grow/cultivate by sowing seeds
2.	分货	fēn huò	phr.	sort goods
3.	拣货量	jiǎnhuòliàng	n.	picking volume
4.	重合度	chónghédù	n.	overlap ratio

补充专业词语　Supplementary Specialized Vocabulary

1.	自动分拣系统	zìdòng fēnjiǎn xìtǒng	phr.	automatic sorting system
2.	节省人力	jiéshěng rénlì	phr.	save manpower
3.	降低货损	jiàngdī huòsǔn	phr.	reduce cargo damage
4.	数据存储	shùjù cúnchǔ	phr.	data storage

播种式拣选
DAS Picking

jùzi
句子
Sentences

1. 播种式拣选是把多个订单汇总成一批,把相同品种的商品数量进行汇总并一起拣选出来,再逐个品种对所有客户进行分货的拣选方法。
2. 播种式拣选一次可以拣选多个订单的货物。
3. 播种式拣选适用于货物品种和数量都比较多、货物重合度较高的情况。

5

Bǔ huò zuòyè
补货作业
Replenishment Operation

bǔ huò zuòyè de liúchéng
补货作业的 流程
the process of replenishment operation

kèhù dìnghuò
客户订货
the customer places an order

dāng cúnhuò bùzú shí, kāishǐ bǔ huò
当 存货不足时, 开始补货
when the goods in stock runs low, start replenishing

bǎ zhuānghǎo huò de tuōpán yóu
把 装好 货的托盘 由
bǎoguǎnqū yízhì jiǎnhuòqū
保管区 移至拣货区
move the loaded pallets from the storage area to the picking area

jiǎnchá jiǎnhuòqū cúnhuò
检查拣货区存货
check the goods in stock in the picking area

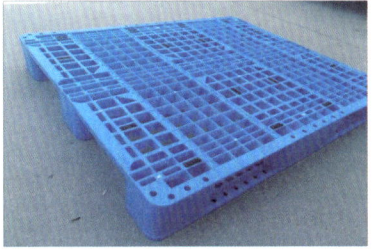

zhǎochū kōng tuōpán
找出 空拖盘
find empty pallets

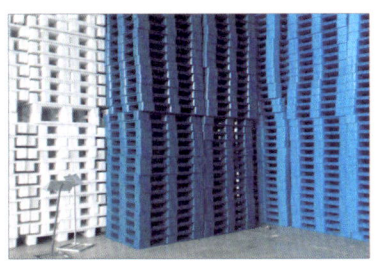

chóng jiàn cúnhuò dàng'àn, bìng jiāng tuōpán guīwèi
重 建存货 档案,并 将托盘归位
recreate the inventory file and replace the pallets

49

题解 Introduction

1. 学习内容：补货作业的定义、种类和流程。
   Learning content: The definition, types and process of replenishment operation.
2. 知识目标：掌握与补货作业相关的核心词语及表达，学习汉字的笔画"㇏""㇂""㇆""乚"和独体结构，学写相关汉字。
   Knowledge objectives: Grasp the core vocabulary and expressions related to replenishment operation, learn the strokes "㇏", "㇂", "㇆", "乚" and independent structure of Chinese characters, and learn to write the related Chinese characters.
3. 技能目标：能在实际工作中完成补货作业。
   Skill objective: Be able to complete replenishment operation in actual work.

第一部分 Part 1

课文 Texts

一、热身 rèshēn Warm-up

1. 给词语选择对应的图片。Choose the corresponding pictures for the words.

A.

B.

C.

D.

① dìbǎn píng zhì duīdié
   地板平置堆叠 _____
   tiered pallet loads

② zhěng xiāng huòjià duīfàng
   整 箱 货架 堆放 _____
   full container loads stacked on the shelves

③ tuōpán bǔ huò
   托盘补货 _____
   pallet replenishment

④ zhěng xiāng bǔ huò
   整 箱 补货 _____
   full container load replenishment

2. 看视频，了解补货作业的种类，并将补货作业的种类与对应的图片连线。**Watch the video to understand the types of replenishment operation and connect the types of replenishment operation to the corresponding pictures.**

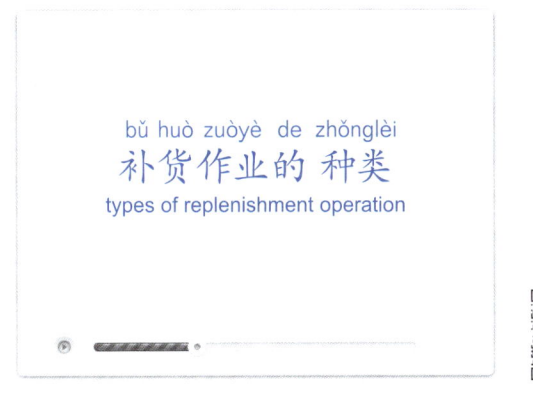

bǔ huò zuòyè de zhǒnglèi
补货作业的 种类
types of replenishment operation

①

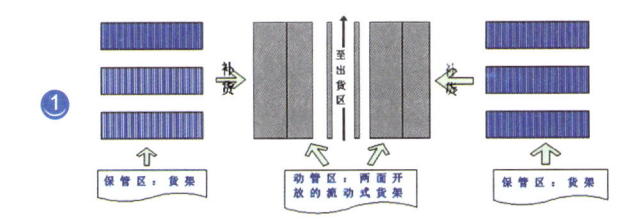

huòjià shàng céng — xià céng de bǔ huò
A. 货架 上 层—下层的补货
replenishment between shelf layers

②

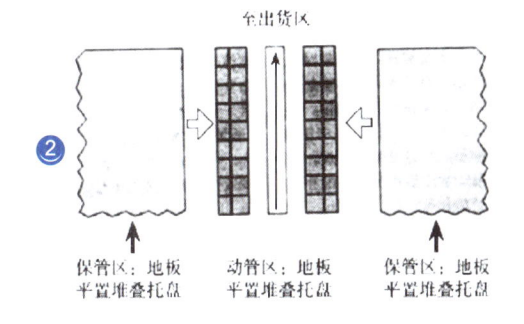

zhěng xiāng bǔ huò
B. 整 箱 补货
full container load replenishment

③

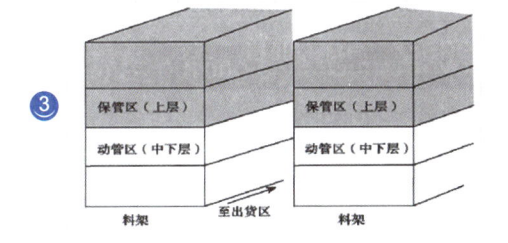

tuōpán bǔ huò
C. 托盘补货
pallet replenishment

二、课文 kèwén Texts

A 🎧 05-01

Bǔ huò zuòyè jiù shì jiāng huòwù cóng cāngkù bǎoguǎnqū bānyùn dào jiǎnhuòqū.
补货作业就是将 货物从 仓库保管区搬运到拣货区。

Tā fēnwéi tuōpán bǔ huò、zhěng xiāng bǔ huò、huòjià shàng céng — xià céng de bǔ huò.
它分为托盘补货、整 箱 补货、货架上 层—下层的补货。

51

译文 yìwén Text in English

The replenishment operation is to move the goods from the storage area in the warehouse to the picking area. It is divided into pallet replenishment, full container load replenishment, and replenishment between shelf layers.

tuōpán bǔ huò
托盘补货
pallet replenishment

zhěng xiāng bǔ huò
整箱补货
full container load replenishment

huòjià shàng céng — xià céng de bǔ huò
货架上层—下层的补货
replenishment between shelf layers

普通词语 pǔtōng cíyǔ General Vocabulary 🎧 05-02

1.	分	fēn	v.	divide, split
2.	为	wéi	v.	become, turn/change into
3.	整	zhěng	adj.	whole
4.	上	shàng	n.	upper position
5.	层	céng	m.	layer, tier
6.	下	xià	n.	lower position

专业词语 zhuānyè cíyǔ Specialized Vocabulary 🎧 05-03

1.	补货	bǔ huò	phr.	replenish goods
2.	保管区	bǎoguǎnqū	n.	storage area
3.	拣货区	jiǎnhuòqū	n.	picking area

B 🎧 05-04

Shìfǒu xūyào bǔ huò zhǔyào kàn jiǎnhuòqū de huòwù cúnliàng.
是否需要补货主要看拣货区的货物存量。

Dāng jiǎnhuòqū huòwù cúnliàng dīyú ānquán cúnliàng shí jiù xūyào bǔ huò.
当拣货区货物存量低于安全存量时就需要补货。

补货作业 5
Replenishment Operation

译文 yìwén Text in English

Whether replenishment is needed mainly depends on the amount of goods in stock in the picking area. Replenishment is needed when the amount of goods in stock in the picking area is below the safety stock.

普通词语 pǔtōng cíyǔ General Vocabulary 🎧 05-05

1.	看	kàn	v.	depend on
2.	当	dāng	prep.	(just) at (a time/place)
3.	低	dī	adj.	low, below the average

专业词语 zhuānyè cíyǔ Specialized Vocabulary 🎧 05-06

存量   cúnliàng   n.   stock

三、视听说 shì-tīng-shuō Viewing, Listening and Speaking

看视频，了解补货作业的流程，并将下列选项按照补货作业的流程排序。**Watch the video to understand the process of replenishment operation and arrange the following options in order of the process of replenishment operation.**

bǔ huò zuòyè de liúchéng
补货作业的流程
process of replenishment operation

❶	zhǎochū kōng tuōpán **找出 空 托盘** find empty pallets
❷	dāng cúnhuò bùzú shí, kāishǐ bǔ huò **当 存货不足时，开始补货** when the goods in stock runs low, start replenishing
❸	bǎ zhuānghǎo huò de tuōpán yóu bǎoguǎnqū yízhì jiǎnhuòqū **把 装好 货的托盘由保管区移至拣货区** move the loaded pallets from the storage area to the picking area
❹	jiǎnchá jiǎnhuòqū cúnhuò **检查拣货区存货** check the goods in stock in the picking area

> chóng jiàn cúnhuò dàng'àn, bìng jiāng tuōpán guīwèi
> ❺ 重建存货档案，并将托盘归位
> recreate the inventory file and replace the pallets

> kèhù dìnghuò
> ❻ 客户订货
> the customer places an order

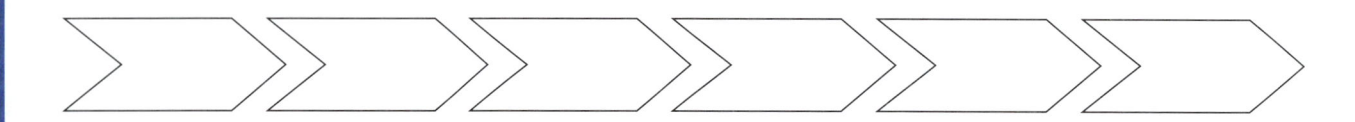

四、学以致用　xuéyǐzhìyòng　Practicing What You Have Learnt

看视频，进一步学习不同补货方式的适用范围，并判断下列情况应该选择哪种补货方式。Watch the video to further learn the scope of application of different replenishment methods and determine which replenishment method should be chosen for the following situations.

bǔ huò fāngshì de xuǎnzé
补货方式的选择
choice of replenishment methods

Rúguǒ yí gè kèhù xūyào 1000 xiāng niúnǎi, kěshì jiǎnhuòqū zhǐ yǒu 10 xiāng le, nǐ juéde yòng nǎ zhǒng bǔ huò
如果一个客户需要1000箱牛奶，可是拣货区只有10箱了，你觉得用哪种补货
fāngshì bǐjiào hǎo ne?
方式比较好呢？

If a customer needs 1000 cartons of milk, but there are only 10 cartons left in the picking area. Which replenishment method do you think is the best?

tuōpán bǔ huò
A. 托盘补货
pallet replenishment

zhěng xiāng bǔ huò
B. 整箱补货
full container load replenishment

huòjià shàng céng — xià céng de bǔ huò
C. 货架上层—下层的补货
replenishment between shelf layers

五、小知识　xiǎo zhīshi　Tips

Guānyú ānquán cúnliàng hé dòngguǎnqū de zhīshi
关于 安全 存量 和 动管区 的知识

Ānquán cúnliàng yě chēng "zuì dī cúnliàng", jí wèile fángzhǐ línshí yòngliàng zēngdà、duìfāng
安全 存量也 称 "最低存量"，即为了防止临时用量 增大、对方
fā huò huò yùnshū wùqī děng, wèi dìnghuò jiàngéqī hé hàoyòngliàng de zēngjiā ér jiànlì de kùcún.
发货或 运输误期等，为 订货间隔期和 耗用量的增加而建立的库存。
Dòngguǎnqū shì yījù rùkùdān xùnsù jiēshòu yùbèiqū huòwù de qūyù hé gēnjù bǔhuòdān bǔhuò shí,
动管区 是依据 入库单迅速接受预备区 货物的 区域和根据补货单补货时，
línshí cúnfàng huòwù de qūyù.
临时存放 货物的 区域。

Knowledge about Safety Stock and Forward Area

The safety stock, also known as the "minimum stock", is the stock established to prevent the temporary consumption from increasing, as well as to prevent delay in delivery or shipment of the other party and to increase the order intervals and consumption. Forward area is the area where the goods in the preparation area are received promptly according to the warehouse entries and where the goods are temporarily stored when replenishing according to the replenishment orders.

第二部分　Part 2
汉字　Chinese Characters

一、汉字知识　Hànzì zhīshi　Knowledge about Chinese Characters

1. 汉字的笔画（5）Strokes of Chinese characters (5)

笔画 Strokes	名称 Names	例字 Examples
㇂	斜钩 xiégōu	我
㇆	卧钩 wògōu	心
㇅	横折钩 héngzhégōu	问
㇈	横折弯钩 héngzhéwāngōu	几

2. 汉字的结构（1）Structures of Chinese characters (1)

结构类型 Structure type	例字 Examples	结构图示 Illustration
独体结构 Independent structure	生 不	□

二、汉字认读与书写　Hànzì rèndú yǔ shūxiě　The Recognition and Writing of Chinese Characters

认读下列词语，并试着读写构成词语的汉字。Recognize the following words, and try to read and write the Chinese characters forming these words.

托盘补货　　拣货区　　存量　　保管区

托				盘				补				货			
拣				货				区				存			
量				保				管				区			

第三部分　Part 3

日常用语　Daily Expressions

❶ 我要两张11号到上海的火车票。Wǒ yào liǎng zhāng 11 hào dào Shànghǎi de huǒchēpiào. I want two train tickets to Shanghai on the 11th.

❷ 我的护照和钱包都丢了。Wǒ de hùzhào hé qiánbāo dōu diū le. I've lost my passport and wallet.

❸ 还可以便宜一些吗？ Hái kěyǐ piányi yìxiē ma? Can it be cheaper?

第四部分　Part 4

单元实训　Unit Practical Training

补货作业应用实训　bǔ huò zuòyè yìngyòng shíxùn
Practical Training of Replenishment Operation Application

实训目的 Training purpose

通过本次实训，了解补货作业的流程。

Through this practical training, understand the process of replenishment operation.

实训组织 Training organization

每组6人。

Each group consists of 6 trainees.

实训步骤 Training steps

❶ 教师提前准备好补货作业流程图，并讲解实训规则。

The teacher prepares the flow diagrams of replenishment operation in advance and explains the training rules.

❷ 教师宣布实训开始，先请第一组的6名组员各抽取一张流程图并快速按补货作业的流程顺序排队。

The teacher announces the beginning of the training, first asks the 6 members of the first group to each draw a flow diagram and queue up in order of the process of replenishment operation quickly.

❸ 教师检查排队是否正确并随机请某位组员读出自己手中牌子上的工作内容，说出是补货作业流程中的第几步以及前、后两个流程是什么。

The teacher checks whether the queue is correct and randomly asks a group member to read out the work content on the flow diagram in his hand, and tell which step it is in the process of replenishment operation, as well as what the preceding and subsequent steps are.

❹ 其余各组依次进行实训。

Other groups take turns to carry out the training.

❺ 教师总结评价，实训结束。

The teacher summarizes and evaluates, and the training ends.

第五部分　Part 5　单元小结 Unit Summary

词语 *cíyǔ* Vocabulary

普通词语　General Vocabulary

1.	分	fēn	v.	divide, split
2.	为	wéi	v.	become, turn/change into
3.	整	zhěng	adj.	whole
4.	上	shàng	n.	upper position
5.	层	céng	m.	layer, tier
6.	下	xià	n.	lower position
7.	看	kàn	v.	depend on
8.	当	dāng	prep.	(just) at (a time/place)
9.	低	dī	adj.	low, below the average

专业词语　Specialized Vocabulary

1.	补货	bǔ huò	phr.	replenish goods
2.	保管区	bǎoguǎnqū	n.	storage area
3.	拣货区	jiǎnhuòqū	n.	picking area
4.	存量	cúnliàng	n.	stock

补充专业词语　Supplementary Specialized Vocabulary

1.	托盘补货	tuōpán bǔ huò	phr.	pallet replenishment
2.	整箱补货	zhěng xiāng bǔ huò	phr.	full container load replenishment
3.	存货档案	cúnhuò dàng'àn	phr.	inventory file

jùzi 句子 Sentences	1. 补货作业就是将货物从仓库保管区搬运到拣货区。 2. 它分为托盘补货、整箱补货、货架上层—下层的补货。 3. 是否需要补货主要看拣货区的货物存量。 4. 当拣货区货物存量低于安全存量时就需要补货。

6

Pèi zhuāng zuòyè
配装作业
Loading Operation

pèi zhuāng zuòyè de yuánzé
配装作业的原则
the principles of loading operation

chōngfèn lìyòng chēliàng yǒuxiào róngjī hé zàizhòngliàng
充分利用车辆有效容积和载重量
make full use of the effective volume and load capacity of vehicles

shìdàng chèn diàn, fángzhǐ huòwù sǔnhuài
适当衬垫，防止货物损坏
pad properly to prevent damage to the goods

jìnzhǐ chāozhòng
禁止超重
do not overload

zhòng bù yā qīng, dà bù yā xiǎo
重不压轻，大不压小
do not place heavy items on light ones, or large items on small ones

zhòngxīn pínghéng
重心平衡
the center of gravity is balanced

biāoqiān cháo wài
标签朝外
the labels face outward

59

> **题解 Introduction**
>
> 1. 学习内容：配装作业的定义、原则和最优方案设计。
>   Learning content: The definition, principles and optical scheme design of loading operation.
> 2. 知识目标：掌握与配装作业相关的核心词语及表达，学习汉字的笔画"㇇""㇈"和品字形结构，学写相关汉字。
>   Knowledge objectives: Grasp the core vocabulary and expressions related to loading operation, learn the strokes "㇇", "㇈" and 品-shaped structure of Chinese characters, and learn to write the related Chinese characters.
> 3. 技能目标：能在实际工作中完成配装作业。
>   Skill objective: Be able to complete loading operation in actual work.

第一部分　Part 1

课文　Texts

一、热身　rèshēn　Warm-up

1. 给词语选择对应的图片。Choose the corresponding pictures for the words.

A.

B.

C.

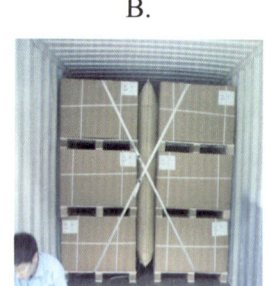

D.

❶ huòwù zhuāng chē
货物 装 车 _____
truck loading

❷ chāozhòng
超重 _____
overload

❸ zhòngxīn pínghéng
重心 平衡 _____
balanced center of gravity

❹ chèn diàn
衬 垫 _____
padding

60

配装作业 6
Loading Operation

2. 看视频，了解配装作业的原则，并将配装作业的原则与对应的图片连线。**Watch the video to understand the principles of loading operation, and connect the principles of loading operation to the corresponding pictures.**

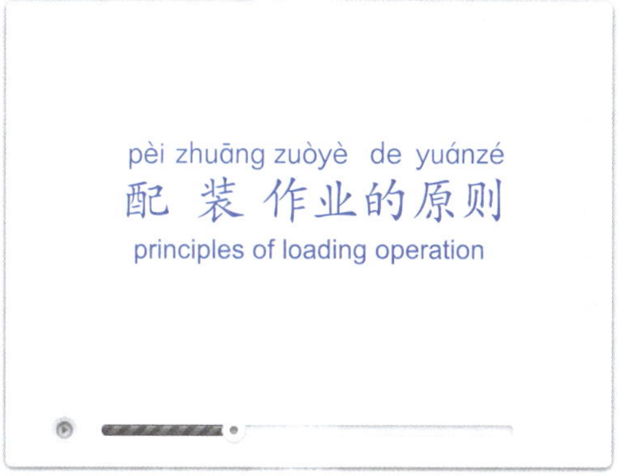

pèi zhuāng zuòyè de yuánzé
配 装 作 业 的 原 则
principles of loading operation

① jìnzhǐ chāozhòng
禁止 超重
do not overload

② chōngfèn lìyòng chēliàng yǒuxiào róngjī hé zàizhòngliàng
充分 利用 车辆 有效 容积 和 载重量
make full use of the effective volume and load capacity of vehicles

③ zhòng bù yā qīng, dà bù yā xiǎo
重 不压轻，大不压小
do not place heavy items on light ones, or large items on small ones

④ shìdàng chèn diàn, fángzhǐ huòwù sǔnhuài
适当 衬垫，防止 货物 损坏
pad properly to prevent damage to the goods

A.

B.

C.

D.

61

biāoqiān cháo wài
❺ 标签 朝 外
the labels face outward

E.

zhòngxīn pínghéng
❻ 重心 平衡
the center of gravity is balanced

F.

二、课文　kèwén　Texts

A 06-01

　　Pèi zhuāng zuòyè shì zhǐ wèile chōngfèn lìyòng yùnshū gōngjù de zàizhòngliàng hé róngjīlǜ,
　　配 装 作业是指为了充分利用运输工具的 载重量 和容积率，
cǎiyòng hélǐ fāngfǎ jìnxíng zhuāngzài.
采用合理方法进行 装载。

　　Dāng huòwù shì xiǎo pīliàng、duō pīcì de shíhou, yào jǐnliàng bǎ tóngyī kèhù de
　　当 货物是小 批量、多批次的时候，要尽量把同一客户的
duō zhǒng huòwù huò duō gè kèhù de huòwù dāpèi jìnxíng zhuāngzài.
多 种 货物或多个客户的货物搭配进行 装载。

译文 yìwén Text in English

　　The loading operation refers to load by adopting a reasonable method to make full use of the load capacity and volume ratio of transport.

　　When the goods are in small quantities and multiple batches, it is necessary to try to load a variety of goods from the same customer or a combination of goods from multiple customers.

普通词语 pǔtōng cíyǔ General Vocabulary 06-02

1.	指	zhǐ	v.	refer to
2.	为了	wèile	prep.	for, in order to
3.	充分	chōngfèn	adj.	full, abundant
4.	利用	lìyòng	v.	make use of, utilize
5.	工具	gōngjù	n.	tool
6.	采用	cǎiyòng	v.	use, adopt
7.	合理	hélǐ	adj.	reasonable

8.	装载	zhuāngzài	v.	(of a vehicle, ship, etc.) carry, load
9.	小	xiǎo	adj.	small
10.	时候	shíhou	n.	(the duration of) time
11.	尽量	jǐnliàng	adv.	as far as possible
12.	同一	tóngyī	adj.	(one and the) same, identical
13.	搭配	dāpèi	v.	arrange according to given requirements, organize in pairs/groups

专业词语 zhuānyè cíyǔ Specialized Vocabulary 06-03

1.	配装	pèi zhuāng	phr.	load
2.	载重量	zàizhòngliàng	n.	load capacity
3.	容积率	róngjīlǜ	n.	volume ratio
4.	批量	pīliàng	n.	size/volume of a batch (of products)
5.	批次	pīcì	m.	batch

B 06-04

Pèisòng zhuāngzài yào chōngfèn lìyòng chēliàng de yǒuxiào róngjī hé zàizhòngliàng.
配送装载要充分利用车辆的有效容积和载重量。

Zhuāngzài shí yào chèn diàn, fángzhǐ huòwù sǔnhuài, jìnzhǐ chāozhòng, zhòng de huòwù
装载时要衬垫，防止货物损坏，禁止超重，重的货物

bù yā qīng de, dà de huòwù bù yā xiǎo de. Huòwù de zhòngxīn yào pínghéng, huòwù de
不压轻的，大的货物不压小的。货物的重心要平衡，货物的

biāoqiān cháo wài.
标签朝外。

译文 yìwén Text in English

Loading should make full use of the effective volume and load capacity of vehicles.

During loading, it is necessary to pad to prevent damage to the goods. Do not overload. Do not place heavy items on light ones, or large items on small ones. The center of gravity of the goods should be balanced, and the labels of the goods should face outward.

普通词语 pǔtōng cíyǔ General Vocabulary 06-05

1.	防止	fángzhǐ	v.	prevent
2.	损坏	sǔnhuài	v.	damage, break
3.	禁止	jìnzhǐ	v.	prohibit, forbid

4.	重	zhòng	adj.	heavy
5.	压	yā	v.	press, crush
6.	轻	qīng	adj.	light, of little weight
7.	重心	zhòngxīn	n.	center of gravity
8.	平衡	pínghéng	adj.	balanced
9.	朝	cháo	v.	face
10.	外	wài	n.	the outside

专业词语 zhuānyè cíyǔ Specialized Vocabulary 🎧 06-06

1.	配送	pèisòng	v.	distribute, deliver
2.	有效容积	yǒuxiào róngjī	phr.	effective volume
3.	衬垫	chèn diàn	phr.	pad
4.	超重	chāo//zhòng	v.	overload

三、视听说 shì-tīng-shuō Viewing, Listening and Speaking

观看介绍货物最优配装方案的视频，说一说设计货物最优配装方案需要知道哪些基本信息。Watch the video introducing the optimal loading scheme and talk about what basic information we need to know to design the optimal loading scheme for goods.

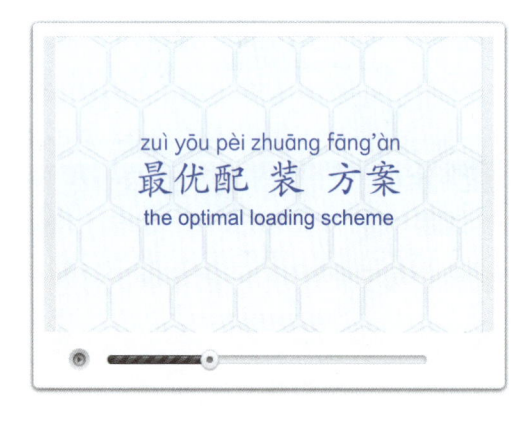

zuì yōu pèi zhuāng fāng'àn
最优配装方案
the optimal loading scheme

A. chēxiāng róngjī
车厢 容积
volume of cargo body

B. huòwù de bāozhuāng
货物的 包装
packing of goods

C. chēxiāng de zàizhòngliàng
车厢的 载重量
load capacity of cargo body

D. huòwù de zhòngliàng
货物的 重量
weight of goods

E. huòwù de xínghào
货物的 型号
models of goods

F. huòwù de tǐjī
货物的体积
volume of goods

shèjì huòwù zuì yōu pèi zhuāng fāng'àn xūyào zhīdào
设计货物最优配装方案需要知道：_____
When designing the optimal loading scheme for goods, you need to know:

四、学以致用　xuéyǐzhìyòng　Practicing What You Have Learnt

看视频，进一步学习如何设计货物最优配装方案，并完成练习。**Watch the video to further learn how to design the optimal loading scheme for goods, and complete the exercises.**

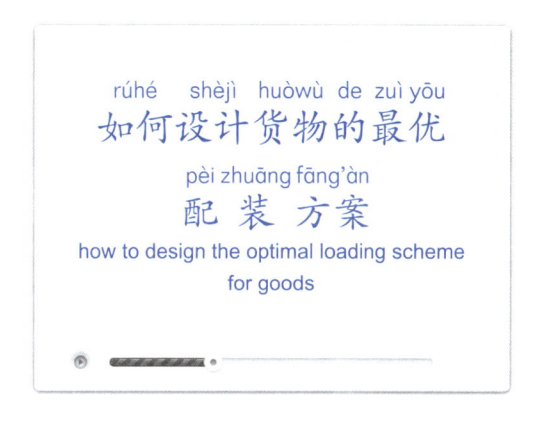

某配送中心某次需配送牛奶和苹果两种货物，牛奶的体积 V1 是 $2m^3/t$，苹果的体积 V2 是 $1m^3/t$，计划使用车辆的载重量 A 是 15t，车厢容积 B 是 $25m^3$。试问牛奶的重量 W1 是多少？苹果的重量 W2 是多少？

A distribution center needs to deliver two types of goods: milk and apples. The volume of milk (V1) is $2m^3/t$, that of apples (V2) is $1m^3/t$, the load capacity of the vehicle planned to be used (A) is 15t, and the volume of cargo body (B) is $25m^3$. What is the weight of milk (W1)? And what is the weight of apples (W2)?

五、小知识　xiǎo zhīshi　Tips

关于有效容积和载重量的知识

有效容积指的是物体实际的容积大小。车辆载重量是指容许装载的最大重量。通常货车有三十吨、四十吨、五十吨、六十吨、九十吨等不同的载重量。

Knowledge about Effective Volume and Load Capacity

The effective volume refers to the actual volume of an object. The load capacity of a vehicle refers to the maximum allowable loaded weight. Usually trucks have different load capacities of 30, 40, 50, 60 and 90 tons.

第二部分　Part 2
汉字　Chinese Characters

一、汉字知识　Hànzì zhīshi　Knowledge about Chinese Characters

1. 汉字的笔画（6）　Strokes of Chinese characters (6)

笔画 Strokes	名称 Names	例字 Examples
ㄋ	横撇弯钩 héngpiěwāngōu	部
ㄋ	横折折折钩 héngzhézhézhégōu	奶

2. 汉字的结构（2）　Structures of Chinese characters (2)

结构类型 Structure type	例字 Example	结构图示 Illustration
品字形结构 品-shaped structure	品	⊞

二、汉字认读与书写　Hànzì rèndú yǔ shūxiě　The Recognition and Writing of Chinese Characters

认读下列词语，并试着读写构成词语的汉字。Recognize the following words, and try to read and write the Chinese characters forming these words.

配装　　载重量　　容积率

配			装			载			重		
量			容			积			率		

第三部分　Part 3
日常用语　Daily Expressions

❶ 请原谅。Qǐng yuánliàng. Pardon me, please./ Forgive me, please.

❷ 不好意思，我没收到你的短信。Bù hǎoyìsi, wǒ méi shōudào nǐ de duǎnxìn. Excuse me, I didn't receive your text message.

❸ 我前几天感冒了。Wǒ qián jǐ tiān gǎnmào le. I had a cold a few days ago.

第四部分　Part 4　单元实训 Unit Practical Training

配装作业应用实训　pèi zhuāng zuòyè yìngyòng shíxùn
Practical Training of Loading Operation Application

实训目的 Training purpose
通过本次实训，了解配装的内涵。
Through this practical training, understand the connotation of loading.

实训组织 Training organization
每组 5 人。
Each group consists of 5 trainees.

实训步骤 Training steps

❶ 教师讲解实训内容：假设水泥的长、宽、高分别是 2m、1m、1m，玻璃的长、宽、高分别是 1m、1m、1m，车厢的长、宽、高分别是 5m、3m、1m，请思考如何堆放货物。
The teacher explains the content of the training: Assuming that the length, width, and height of the cement are 2m, 1m, and 1m respectively, the length, width, and height of the glass are 1m, 1m, and 1m respectively, and the length, width, and height of the cargo body are 5m, 3m, and 1m respectively, please think about how to stack these goods.

❷ 教师宣布实训开始，每组分别进行设计。
The teacher announces the beginning of the training, and each group designs their schemes separately.

❸ 每组选派 1 名组员讲解设计方案。
Each group selects a member to explain the design scheme.

❹ 教师总结评价，实训结束。
The teacher summarizes and evaluates, and the training ends.

第五部分　Part 5　单元小结 Unit Summary

普通词语　General Vocabulary

cíyǔ
词语 Vocabulary

1.	指	zhǐ	v.	refer to
2.	为了	wèile	prep.	for, in order to
3.	充分	chōngfèn	adj.	full, abundant
4.	利用	lìyòng	v.	make use of, utilize
5.	工具	gōngjù	n.	tool
6.	采用	cǎiyòng	v.	use, adopt
7.	合理	hélǐ	adj.	reasonable

词语 cíyǔ Vocabulary

8.	装载	zhuāngzài	v.	(of a vehicle, ship, etc.) carry, load
9.	小	xiǎo	adj.	small
10.	时候	shíhou	n.	(the duration of) time
11.	尽量	jǐnliàng	adv.	as far as possible
12.	同一	tóngyī	adj.	(one and the) same, identical
13.	搭配	dāpèi	v.	arrange according to given requirements, organize in pairs/groups
14.	防止	fángzhǐ	v.	prevent
15.	损坏	sǔnhuài	v.	damage, break
16.	禁止	jìnzhǐ	v.	prohibit, forbid
17.	重	zhòng	adj.	heavy
18.	压	yā	v.	press, crush
19.	轻	qīng	adj.	light, of little weight
20.	重心	zhòngxīn	n.	center of gravity
21.	平衡	pínghéng	adj.	balanced
22.	朝	cháo	v.	face
23.	外	wài	n.	the outside

专业词语 Specialized Vocabulary

1.	配装	pèi zhuāng	phr.	load
2.	载重量	zàizhòngliàng	n.	load capacity
3.	容积率	róngjīlǜ	n.	volume ratio
4.	批量	pīliàng	n.	size/volume of a batch (of products)
5.	批次	pīcì	m.	batch
6.	配送	pèisòng	v.	distribute, deliver
7.	有效容积	yǒuxiào róngjī	phr.	effective volume
8.	衬垫	chèn diàn	phr.	pad
9.	超重	chāo//zhòng	v.	overload

补充专业词语 Supplementary Specialized Vocabulary

	体积	tǐjī	n.	volume, size

句子 jùzi Sentences

1. 配装作业是指为了充分利用运输工具的载重量和容积率，采用合理方法进行装载。
2. 配送装载要充分利用车辆的有效容积和载重量。

7 退货作业
Tuìhuò zuòyè
Return Operation

tuìhuò zuòyè de liúchéng
退货作业的 流程
the process of return operation

tuìhuò yànshōu zuòyè
退货 验收 作业
acceptance operation of returned goods

liángpǐn rù kù zuòyè
良品 入库作业
inbound operation of good products

bùliángpǐn tuìhuò zuòyè: bùliángpǐn yíjiāo
不良品退货作业：不良品移交
gōngyìngshāng, gōngyìngshāng shěnhé tuìhuò
供应商， 供应商 审核退货
return operation of defective products: defective products are handed over to the supplier, and the supplier reviews the returned goods

tuìhuò zhěnglǐ zuòyè
退货 整理作业
sorting out operation of returned goods

jù shōu tuì zuòyè
拒 收退作业
rejection operation of returned goods

69

题解 Introduction

1. 学习内容：退货作业的定义、流程、退货原因以及拒绝退货的情况。
   Learning content: The definition and process of return operation, reasons for returning goods and circumstances in which a customer's return request may be rejected.

2. 知识目标：掌握与退货作业相关的核心词语及表达，学习汉字的笔画"ㄅ""ㄟ"和上下结构、上中下结构，学写相关汉字。
   Knowledge objectives: Grasp the core vocabulary and expressions related to return operation, learn the strokes "ㄅ", "ㄟ", top-bottom structure and top-middle-bottom structure of Chinese characters, and learn to write the related Chinese characters.

3. 技能目标：能在实际工作中完成退货作业。
   Skill objective: Be able to complete return operation in actual work.

第一部分 Part 1

课文 Texts

一、热身 rèshēn Warm-up

1. 给词语选择对应的图片。Choose the corresponding pictures for the words.

A.

B.

C.

D.

① guòqī
过期 _____
expired

② jiǎ huò
假货 _____
fake goods

③ cìpǐn
次品 _____
defective goods

④ sǔnhuài
损坏 _____
damaged

退货作业 7
Return Operation

2. 看视频，了解退货的原因，并将退货原因与对应的图片连线。**Watch the video to understand the reasons for returning goods, and connect them to the corresponding pictures.**

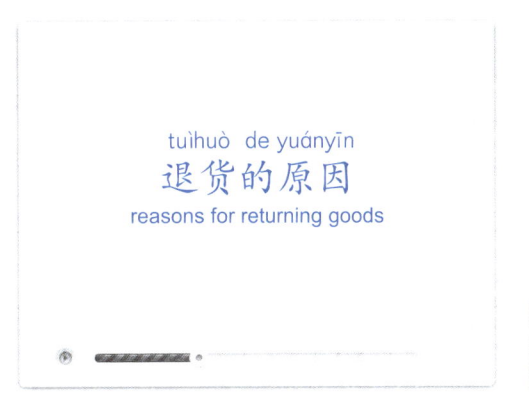

tuìhuò de yuányīn
退货的原因
reasons for returning goods

①

shāngpǐn guòqī
A. 商品过期
goods expired

②

cìpǐn huíshōu
B. 次品回收
recycling defective goods

③

bānyùn zhōng sǔnhuài
C. 搬运中损坏
damaged during handling

④

yǒu zhìliàng wèntí
D. 有质量问题
having quality problems

71

二、课文 kèwén Texts

A 07-01

Tuìhuò shì zhǐ zài pèisòng huódòng zhōng, yóuyú pèisòng zhōngxīn huòzhě yònghù duì pèisòng
退货是指在配送 活动 中，由于配送 中心 或者用户对配送
de huòwù cúnzài yìyì, jiāng huòwù tuìhuí pèisòng zhōngxīn jìnxíng chǔlǐ de yí xiàng huódòng.
的货物存在异议，将 货物退回配送 中心 进行处理的一项 活动。

译文 yìwén Text in English

Returning goods refers to an activity in which the goods are returned to the distribution center for processing due to the distribution center or the user has objections to the goods distributed during the distribution activity.

普通词语 pǔtōng cíyǔ General Vocabulary 07-02

1.	活动	huódòng	n.	activity
2.	中	zhōng	n.	the inside, being within a certain range/sphere
3.	由于	yóuyú	conj.	because of, due to
4.	或者	huòzhě	conj.	or
5.	用户	yònghù	n.	user, customer
6.	存在	cúnzài	v.	exist
7.	异议	yìyì	n.	objection, disagreement
8.	退回	tuìhuí	v.	return, send back
9.	项	xiàng	m.	*used of itemized things*

专业词语 zhuānyè cíyǔ Specialized Vocabulary 07-03

| 1. | 退货 | tuì//huò | v. | return goods |
| 2. | 中心 | zhōngxīn | n. | center |

退货作业
Return Operation

B 07-04

Shìfǒu xūyào tuìhuò zhǔyào kàn shāngpǐn shìfǒu yǒu zhìliàng wèntí, bānyùn zhōng shìfǒu yǒu sǔnhuài, shāngpǐn shìfǒu guòqī, yǐjí shìfǒu shì cìpǐn děng.

是否需要退货主要看商品是否有质量问题，搬运中是否有损坏，商品是否过期，以及是否是次品等。

译文 yìwén Text in English

Whether the goods need to be returned or not mainly depends on whether the goods have quality problems, whether they are damaged during handling, whether they have expired, and whether they are defective products, etc.

普通词语 pǔtōng cíyǔ General Vocabulary   07-05

| 1. | 问题 | wèntí | n. | problem, question |
| 2. | 以及 | yǐjí | conj. | and |

专业词语 zhuānyè cíyǔ Specialized Vocabulary   07-06

| 1. | 过期 | guò//qī | v. | expire |
| 2. | 次品 | cìpǐn | n. | defective product, defective goods |

三、视听说 shì-tīng-shuō Viewing, Listening and Speaking

看视频，了解拒绝客户退货要求的几种情况，并与对应的图片连线。Watch the video to understand several circumstances in which a customer's return request may be rejected, and connect them to the corresponding pictures.

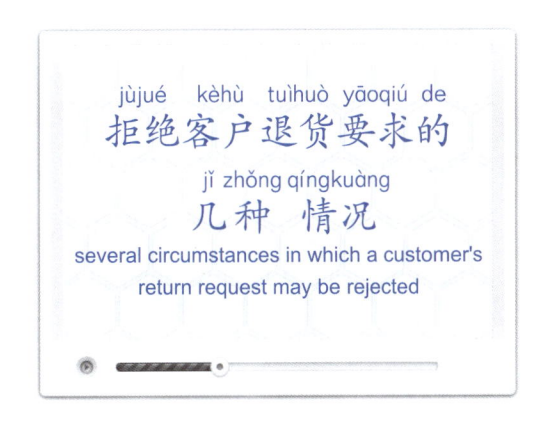

jùjué kèhù tuìhuò yāoqiú de
拒绝客户退货要求的
jǐ zhǒng qíngkuàng
几种情况
several circumstances in which a customer's return request may be rejected

中文+物流管理（中级）

　　　　　　　　　　　　　　　fāpiào、　shōujù diūshī
A. 发票、收据丢失
the invoice or receipt has been lost

　　　　　　　　　　chāoguò guīdìng tuìhuò shíjiān
B. 超过 规定退货时间
the stipulated return time limit has been exceeded

　　　　　　　suǒ tuì shāngpǐn shùliàng búgòu、wàiguān shòusǔn
C. 所退 商品 数量 不够、外观 受损
the quantity of the returned goods is insufficient or the appearance is damaged

四、学以致用　xuéyǐzhìyòng　Practicing What You Have Learnt

看视频，了解退货作业的流程，并将下列选项按照流程的先后顺序排序。**Watch the video to understand the process of return operation and arrange the following options in order of the process.**

tuìhuò zuòyè de liúchéng
退货作业的流程
process of return operation

liángpǐn rù kù zuòyè
❶ 良品入库作业
inbound operation of good products

bùliángpǐn tuìhuò zuòyè
❷ 不良品退货作业
return operation of defective products

tuìhuò yànshōu zuòyè
❸ 退货验收作业
acceptance operation of returned goods

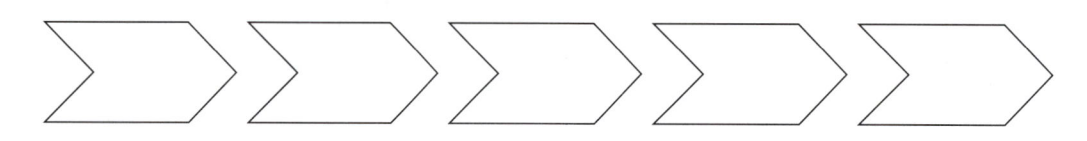

jù shōu tuì zuòyè
❹ 拒收退作业
rejection operation of returned goods

tuìhuò zhěnglǐ zuòyè
❺ 退货整理作业
sorting out operation of returned goods

五、小知识　xiǎo zhīshi　Tips

Guānyú yǒuxiàoqī hé cìpǐn de zhīshi
关于有效期和次品的知识

Yǒuxiàoqī shì zhǐ zài guīdìng de zhùcáng tiáojiàn xià zhìliàng fúhé guīdìng yāoqiú de qīxiàn.
有效期是指在规定的贮藏条件下质量符合规定要求的期限。

Cìpǐn shì zhǐ shēngchǎn qǐyè zài shēngchǎn guòchéng zhōng chǎnshēng de yǒu yánzhòng quēxiàn huòzhě dá bú dào chūkǒu hétóng biāozhǔn、wúfǎ fù chūkǒu de zhìpǐn (bāokuò wánchéngpǐn hé wèiwánchéngpǐn).
次品是指生产企业在生产过程中产生的有严重缺陷或者达不到出口合同标准、无法复出口的制品（包括完成品和未完成品）。

Knowledge about Expiry Date and Defective Products

The expiry date refers to the period during which the quality meets the specified requirements under the specified storage conditions.

The defective products refer to the products (including finished products and unfinished products) produced by the manufacturer in the process of production which are seriously defective or fail to meet the standards of export contract and cannot be re-exported.

第二部分　Part 2
汉字　Chinese Characters

一、汉字知识　Hànzì zhīshi　Knowledge about Chinese Characters

1. 汉字的笔画（7） Strokes of Chinese characters (7)

笔画 Strokes	名称 Names	例字 Examples
㇉	竖折折钩 shùzhézhégōu	马
㇂	横斜钩 héngxiégōu	风

2. 汉字的结构（3） Structures of Chinese characters (3)

结构类型 Structure types	例字 Examples	结构图示 Illustrations
上下结构 Top-bottom structure	爸 节	日
上中下结构 Top-middle-bottom structure	意	三

75

二、汉字认读与书写　Hànzì rèndú yǔ shūxiě　The Recognition and Writing of Chinese Characters

认读下列词语，并试着读写构成词语的汉字。Recognize the following words, and try to read and write the Chinese characters forming these words.

配送　中心　过期　次品

| 配 | | | 送 | | | 中 | | | 心 | | |
| 过 | | | 期 | | | 次 | | | 品 | | |

第三部分　Part 3　日常用语 Daily Expressions

① 麻烦你替我请个假。Máfan nǐ tì wǒ qǐng gè jià. Would you please ask for a leave for me?

② 我被骗了。Wǒ bèi piàn le. I was cheated.

③ 别着急。Bié zháojí. Don't worry.

第四部分　Part 4　单元实训 Unit Practical Training

退货作业应用实训　tuìhuò zuòyè yìngyòng shíxùn
Practical Training of Return Operation Application

实训目的 Training purpose

通过本次实训，了解退货作业的流程。

Through this practical training, understand the process of return operation.

实训组织 Training organization

每组 5 人。

Each group consists of 5 trainees.

实训步骤 Training steps

① 教师提前准备好写着退货作业流程的牌子，并讲解实训规则。

The teacher prepares boards with the process of return operation in advance, and explains the training rules.

② 教师宣布实训开始，第一组的 5 位组员各从教师手中抽取一个牌子，按退货作业流程顺序快速排队。

The teacher announces the beginning of the training, the 5 members of the first group each draws a board from the teacher's hands, and queue up in order of the process of return operation quickly.

退货作业
Return Operation
7

❸ 教师随机请某位组员读出自己手中牌子上的工作内容，说出是退货作业流程的第几步，并说出前、后两个流程分别是什么。
The teacher randomly asks a group member to read out the work content on the board in his hand, and tell which step it is in the process of return operation, as well as what the preceding and subsequent steps are.

❹ 其余各组依次进行实训。
Other groups take turns to carry out the training.

❺ 教师总结评价，实训结束。
The teacher summarizes and evaluates, and the training ends.

第五部分　Part 5　单元小结 Unit Summary

cíyǔ 词语 Vocabulary

普通词语　General Vocabulary

1.	活动	huódòng	n.	activity
2.	中	zhōng	n.	the inside, being within a certain range/sphere
3.	由于	yóuyú	conj.	because of, due to
4.	或者	huòzhě	conj.	or
5.	用户	yònghù	n.	user, customer
6.	存在	cúnzài	v.	exist
7.	异议	yìyì	n.	objection, disagreement
8.	退回	tuìhuí	v.	return, send back
9.	项	xiàng	m.	*used of itemized things*
10.	问题	wèntí	n.	problem, question
11.	以及	yǐjí	conj.	and

专业词语　Specialized Vocabulary

1.	退货	tuì//huò	v.	return goods
2.	中心	zhōngxīn	n.	center
3.	过期	guò//qī	v.	expire
4.	次品	cìpǐn	n.	defective product, defective goods

补充专业词语　Supplementary Specialized Vocabulary

1.	发票	fāpiào	n.	invoice
2.	收据	shōujù	n.	receipt

77

jùzi 句子 Sentences	1. 退货是指在配送活动中,由于配送中心或者用户对配送的货物存在异议,将货物退回配送中心进行处理的一项活动。 2. 是否需要退货主要看商品是否有质量问题,搬运中是否有损坏,商品是否过期,以及是否是次品等。

8

Yùnshū diàodù
运输调度
Transportation Scheduling

yùnshū diàodù de liúchéng
运输调度的流程
the process of transportation scheduling

kèhù yùyuē
客户预约
the customer makes a reservation

diàodùyuán gēnjù liǎojiě de yòng chē xìnxī
调度员根据了解的用车信息
hélǐ ānpái chēliàng
合理安排车辆
the dispatcher arranges the vehicles reasonably based on the known vehicle information

huòwù jiāo huò chǔlǐ
货物交货处理
goods delivery processing

diàodùyuán liǎojiě yòng chē xìnxī
调度员了解用车信息
the dispatcher understands the vehicle information

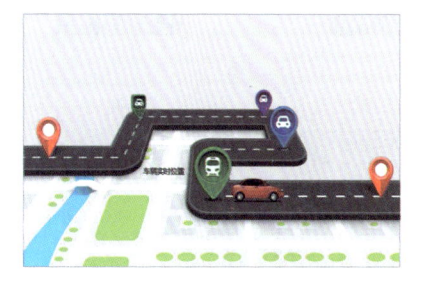

diàodùyuán jiānkòng chēliàng xíngshǐ
调度员监控车辆行驶
the dispatcher monitors vehicle traveling

79

题解　Introduction

1. 学习内容：运输调度信息的内容以及车辆管理系统、安全行驶报警系统的功能。
   Learning content: The content of transportation scheduling information and the functions of vehicle management system and safe driving alarm system.
2. 知识目标：掌握与运输调度相关的核心词语及表达，学习汉字的笔画"⺄""⺆"和左右结构、左中右结构，学写相关汉字。
   Knowledge objectives: Grasp the core vocabulary and expressions related to transportation scheduling, learn the strokes "⺄","⺆", left-right structure and left-middle-right structure of Chinese characters, and learn to write the related Chinese characters.
3. 技能目标：能在实际工作中正确使用车辆管理系统、安全行驶报警系统。
   Skill objective: Be able to correctly use vehicle management system and safe driving alarm system in actual work.

第一部分　Part 1

课文　Texts

一、热身　rèshēn　Warm-up

1. 给词语选择对应的图片。Choose the corresponding pictures for the words.

A.

B.

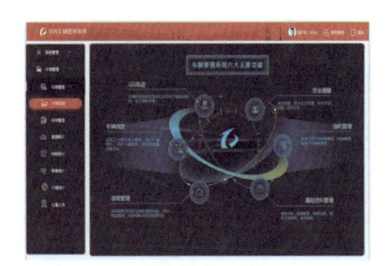

C.

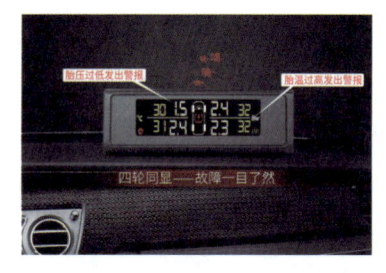

D.

❶ ānquán xíngshǐ bàojǐng xìtǒng
　安全 行驶 报警 系统＿＿＿＿
　safe driving alarm system

❷ chēliàng guǎnlǐ xìtǒng
　车辆 管理 系统＿＿＿＿
　vehicle management system

❸ xíngchē jìlùyí
　行车 记录仪＿＿＿＿
　dashcam

❹ GPS dǎohángyí
　GPS 导航仪＿＿＿＿
　GPS navigator

80

运输调度 8
Transportation Scheduling

2. 看视频，学习运输调度的主要内容，并将下列选项与对应的图片连线。**Watch the video to learn the main content of transportation scheduling, and connect the following options to the corresponding pictures.**

yùnshū diàodù gōngzuò
运输调度工作
transportation scheduling work

① [map image]

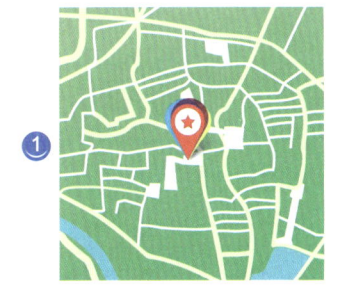

A. chēliàng yāoqiú
车辆 要求
requirements for the vehicle

② [truck image]

B. liánxìrén
联系人
contact person

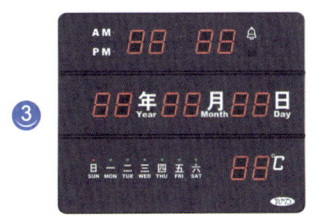

③ [clock/calendar image]

C. shíjiān
时间
time

④ [phone/contact image]

D. zhuǎnhuòdì
转货地
place to trans-ship the cargo

81

二、课文 kèwén Texts

A 🎧 08-01

Chēliàng guǎnlǐ xìtǒng kěyǐ jiānkòng měi liàng chē de yùnxíng guǐjì, kěyǐ tíqián yùyuē
车辆管理系统可以监控每辆车的运行轨迹，可以提前预约

chēliàng, hái kěyǐ xiàng chéngyùnshāng fāsòng chēliàng yùyuē tíxǐng, chéngyùnshāng kěyǐ zhíjiē
车辆，还可以向承运商发送车辆预约提醒，承运商可以直接

zài xìtǒng zhōng huífù.
在系统中回复。

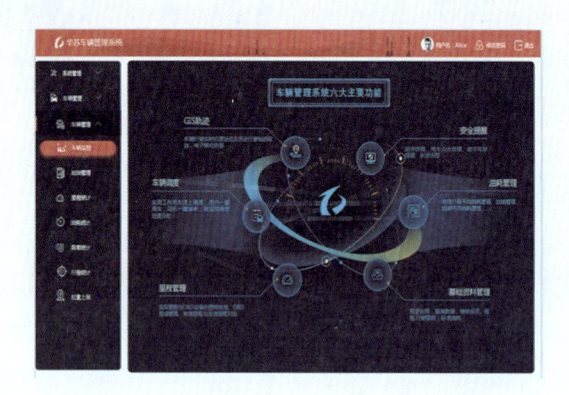

译文 yìwén Text in English

The vehicle management system can monitor the movement trajectory of each vehicle, reserve vehicles in advance, and send reminders of vehicle reservation to the carrier, who can reply directly in the system.

普通词语 pǔtōng cíyǔ General Vocabulary 🎧 08-02

1.	监控	jiānkòng	v.	monitor
2.	辆	liàng	m.	*used with vehicles*
3.	运行	yùnxíng	v.	move
4.	轨迹	guǐjì	n.	trajectory
5.	提前	tíqián	v.	do (sth.) in advance / ahead of time
6.	预约	yùyuē	v.	reserve
7.	发送	fāsòng	v.	send
8.	提醒	tí//xǐng	v.	remind
9.	回复	huífù	v.	reply

8 运输调度 Transportation Scheduling

专业词语 zhuānyè cíyǔ Specialized Vocabulary 🎧 08-03

1.	车辆管理系统	chēliàng guǎnlǐ xìtǒng	phr.	vehicle management system
	系统	xìtǒng	n.	system
2.	承运商	chéngyùnshāng	n.	carrier

B 🎧 08-04

Měi liàng yùnshūchē shang dōu ānzhuāngle xíngchē jìlùyí、GPS dǎohángyí, hái ānzhuāngle ānquán xíngshǐ bàojǐng xìtǒng. Ānquán xíngshǐ bàojǐng xìtǒng jùyǒu píláo jiàshǐ bàojǐng hé chāosù xíngshǐ bàojǐng de gōngnéng.

每辆运输车上都安装了行车记录仪、GPS导航仪，还安装了安全行驶报警系统。安全行驶报警系统具有疲劳驾驶报警和超速行驶报警的功能。

译文 yìwén Text in English

Each transport vehicle is equipped with a dashcam, a GPS navigator, and a safe driving alarm system. The safe driving alarm system has the functions of fatigue driving alarm and speeding alarm.

普通词语 pǔtōng cíyǔ General Vocabulary 🎧 08-05

1.	安装	ānzhuāng	v.	install
2.	具有	jùyǒu	v.	have, possess
3.	疲劳	píláo	adj.	tired, fatigued
4.	驾驶	jiàshǐ	v.	drive
5.	超速	chāosù	v.	exceed the speed limit

专业词语 zhuānyè cíyǔ Specialized Vocabulary 🎧 08-06

1.	行车记录仪	xíngchē jìlùyí	phr.	dashcam
	记录	jìlù	v.	record
2.	导航仪	dǎohángyí	n.	navigator

	导航	dǎoháng	v.	navigate
3.	安全行驶报警系统	ānquán xíngshǐ bàojǐng xìtǒng	phr.	safe driving alarm system
	行驶	xíngshǐ	v.	drive
	报警	bào//jǐng	v.	report (a danger, ect.) to the police or public authorities, give an alarm

三、视听说　shì-tīng-shuō　Viewing, Listening and Speaking

看视频，了解车辆管理系统的功能，并将图片与对应的功能连线。**Watch the video to understand the functions of the vehicle management system, and connect the pictures to the corresponding functions.**

chēliàng guǎnlǐ xìtǒng de gōngnéng
车辆管理系统的 功能
functions of the vehicle management system

①

　　　　　　kěyǐ　zìdòng xiàng chéngyùnshāng fāsòng chēliàng
A. 可以自动 向　承运商　发送 车辆
　　yùyuē tíxǐng
　预约提醒

can automatically send a vehicle reservation reminder to the carrier

②

　　　　kěyǐ　shíshí jiānkòng měi liàng chē de yùnxíng
B. 可以实时 监控 每 辆 车 的 运行
　　　　　　　　　　　guǐjì
　轨迹

can monitor the movement trajectory of each vehicle in real time

③

　　yùnshūliàng dà de shíhou,　kěyǐ　tíqián yùyuē
C. 运输量 大 的 时候，可以 提前 预约
　　chēliàng
　车辆

when the freight volume is large, the system can reserve vehicles in advance

84

四、学以致用　xuéyǐzhìyòng　Practicing What You Have Learnt

看视频，了解运输调度的流程，并将下列选项按照流程的先后顺序排序。Watch the video to understand the process of transportation scheduling, and arrange the following options in order of the process.

yùnshū diàodù de liúchéng
运输调度的流程
process of transportation scheduling

❶	diàodùyuán jiānkòng chēliàng xíngshǐ 调度员 监控 车辆 行驶 the dispatcher monitors vehicle traveling
❷	diàodùyuán gēnjù liǎojiě de yòng chē xìnxī hélǐ ānpái chēliàng 调度员根据了解的用车信息合理安排车辆 the dispatcher arranges the vehicles reasonably based on the known vehicle information
❸	huòwù jiāo huò chǔlǐ 货物交货处理 goods delivery processing
❹	diàodùyuán liǎojiě yòng chē xìnxī 调度员了解用车信息 the dispatcher understands the vehicle information
❺	kèhù yùyuē 客户预约 the customer makes a reservation

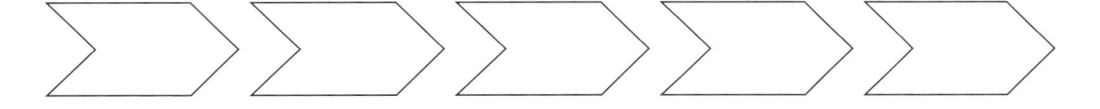

五、小知识　xiǎo zhīshi　Tips

Guānyú ānquán xíngshǐ bàojǐng xìtǒng de zhīshi
关于安全行驶报警系统的知识

Ānquán xíngshǐ bàojǐng xìtǒng tōngcháng jùyǒu píláo jiàshǐ bàojǐng hé chāosù xíngshǐ bàojǐng de
安全行驶报警系统通常具有疲劳驾驶报警和超速行驶报警的

gōngnéng.
功能。

Dì-yī, chēliàng zhuāng yǒu píláo jiàshǐ bàojǐngqì, sījī liánxù jiàshǐ chāoguò 4 xiǎoshí
第一，车辆装有疲劳驾驶报警器，司机连续驾驶超过4小时

bìxū xiūxi yíxiàr, fǒuzé jiù huì bàojǐng.
必须休息一下儿，否则就会报警。

Dì-èr, chēliàng zhuāng yǒu chāosù xíngshǐ bàojǐngqì, rúguǒ chēliàng de sùdù chāoguò
第二，车辆装有超速行驶报警器，如果车辆的速度超过

gōnglù de xiànsù, chāosù xíngshǐ bàojǐngqì yě huì fāchū jǐngbào.
公路的限速，超速行驶报警器也会发出警报。

Knowledge about Safe Driving Alarm System

The safe driving alarm system usually has the functions of fatigue driving alarm and speeding alarm.

First, the vehicle is equipped with a fatigue driving alarm apparatus. The driver must take a rest after driving continuously for more than 4 hours, otherwise it will sound an alarm.

Second, the vehicle is equipped with a speeding alarm apparatus. If the vehicle's speed exceeds the highway speed limit, it will also sound an alarm.

第二部分 Part 2
汉字 Chinese Characters

一、汉字知识 Hànzì zhīshi Knowledge about Chinese Characters

1. 汉字的笔画（8） **Strokes of Chinese characters (8)**

笔画 Strokes	名称 Names	例字 Examples
ㄣ	竖弯 shùwān	四
ㄟ	横折弯 héngzhéwān	没

2. 汉字的结构（4） **Structures of Chinese characters (4)**

结构类型 Structure types	例字 Examples	结构图示 Illustrations
左右结构 Left-right structure	银 饭	⊟
左中右结构 Left-middle-right structure	班 微	⊞

二、汉字认读与书写　Hànzì rèndú yǔ shūxiě　The Recognition and Writing of Chinese Characters

认读下列词语，并试着读写构成词语的汉字。Recognize the following words, and try to read and write the Chinese characters forming these words.

承运商　　车辆管理系统　　调度员

承			运			商			车		
辆			管			理			系		
统			调			度			员		

第三部分 Part 3　日常用语 Daily Expressions

1. 你不能这样。Nǐ bù néng zhèyàng. You can't do this.
2. 我马上就到。Wǒ mǎshàng jiù dào. I will be there right away.
3. 让我想想。Ràng wǒ xiǎngxiang. Let me think about it.

第四部分 Part 4　单元实训 Unit Practical Training

车辆管理系统应用实训　chēliàng guǎnlǐ xìtǒng yìngyòng shíxùn
Practical Training of Vehicle Management System Application

实训目的 Training purpose
通过本次实训，了解车辆管理系统的功能。
Through this practical training, understand the functions of vehicle management system.

实训组织 Training organization
每组4人。
Each group consists of 4 trainees.

实训步骤 Training steps
1. 打开手机或电脑，上网查询车辆管理系统的功能。
   Turn on the mobile phone or computer, inquire about the functions of the vehicle management system on the internet.
2. 每人说出2～3个车辆管理的功能。
   Each trainee names 2-3 functions of vehicle management.

车辆管理系统功能示意图

❸ 小组讨论车辆管理系统还可增加哪些功能并选一名代表发言。
Each group discusses what other functions can be added to the vehicle management system and chooses a representative to speak.

❹ 教师总结评价，实训结束。
The teacher summarizes and evaluates, and the training ends.

第五部分　Part 5　单元小结　Unit Summary

cíyǔ 词语 Vocabulary

普通词语　General Vocabulary

1.	监控	jiānkòng	v.	monitor
2.	辆	liàng	m.	*used with vehicles*
3.	运行	yùnxíng	v.	move
4.	轨迹	guǐjì	n.	trajectory
5.	提前	tíqián	v.	do (sth.) in advance/ahead of time
6.	预约	yùyuē	v.	reserve
7.	发送	fāsòng	v.	send
8.	提醒	tí//xǐng	v.	remind
9.	回复	huífù	v.	reply
10.	安装	ānzhuāng	v.	install
11.	具有	jùyǒu	v.	have, possess
12.	疲劳	píláo	adj.	tired, fatigued
13.	驾驶	jiàshǐ	v.	drive
14.	超速	chāosù	v.	exceed the speed limit

专业词语　Specialized Vocabulary

1.	车辆管理系统	chēliàng guǎnlǐ xìtǒng	phr.	vehicle management system
	系统	xìtǒng	n.	system
2.	承运商	chéngyùnshāng	n.	carrier
3.	行车记录仪	xíngchē jìlùyí	phr.	dashcam
	记录	jìlù	v.	record
4.	导航仪	dǎohángyí	n.	navigator
	导航	dǎoháng	v.	navigate
5.	安全行驶报警系统	ānquán xíngshǐ bàojǐng xìtǒng	phr.	safe driving alarm system
	行驶	xíngshǐ	v.	drive
	报警	bào//jǐng	v.	report (a danger, etc.) to the police or public authorities, give an alarm

运输调度
Transportation Scheduling 8

cíyǔ 词语 Vocabulary

补充专业词语　Supplementary Specialized Vocabulary

1.	调度	diàodù	v.	manage, dispatch
2.	调度员	diàodùyuán	n.	dispatcher
3.	转货地	zhuǎnhuòdì	n.	place to trans-ship cargo

jùzi 句子 Sentences

1. 车辆管理系统可以监控每辆车的运行轨迹，可以提前预约车辆，还可以向承运商发送车辆预约提醒，承运商可以直接在系统中回复。
2. 每辆运输车上都安装了行车记录仪、GPS导航仪，还安装了安全行驶报警系统。
3. 安全行驶报警系统具有疲劳驾驶报警和超速行驶报警的功能。

89

9

Tiáomǎ jìshù
条码技术
Bar Code Technology

èrwéimǎ shēngchéng guòchéng
二维码 生成 过程
the two-dimensional bar code generation process

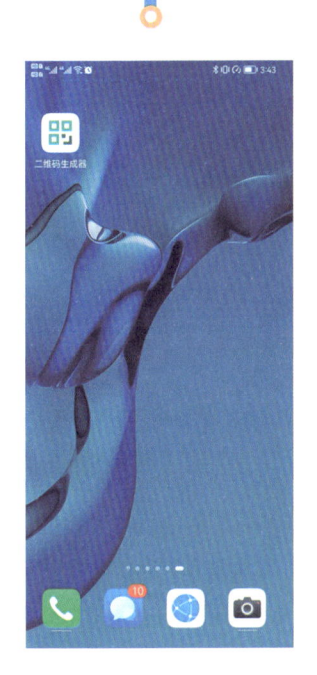

dǎkāi èrwéimǎ shēngchéngqì
打开二维码生成器
open the two-dimensional bar code generator

shūrù shāngpǐn de jīběn xìnxī, bāokuò shāngpǐn míngchēng、jiàgé、chǎngjiā、túpiàn děng zīliào
输入商品的基本信息，包括商品名称、价格、厂家、图片等资料
input the basic information of the commodity, including the commodity name, price, manufacturer, picture, etc.

tiāoxuǎn xíngzhuàng、yánsè děng
挑选形状、颜色等
choose the shape, color, etc.

diǎnjī wánchéng
点击完成
click completed

题解 Introduction

1. 学习内容：一维码和二维码的作用、区别和特性。
   Learning content: The functions of one-dimensional bar codes and two-dimensional bar codes, the difference between them and their characteristics.
2. 知识目标：掌握与一维码和二维码相关的核心词语及表达，学习汉字的笔画"⼺""乚"和全包围结构、半包围结构，学写相关汉字。
   Knowledge objectives: Grasp the core vocabulary and expressions related to one-dimensional bar codes and two-dimensional bar codes, learn the strokes "⼺", "乚", fully-enclosed structure and semi-enclosed structure of Chinese characters, and learn to write the related Chinese characters.
3. 技能目标：能在生活和物流管理中实际运用条码技术。
   Skill objective: Be able to use bar code technology in life and logistics management.

第一部分 Part 1

课文 Texts

一、热身 rèshēn Warm-up

1. 给词语选择对应的图片。Choose the corresponding pictures for the words.

A.

B.

C.

D.

① shāngpǐn tiáomǎ
商品 条码 _____
commodity bar code

② èrwéimǎ
二维码 _____
two-dimensional bar code

③ sǎomiáo yīwéi tiáoxíngmǎ
扫描一维条形码 _____
scan one-dimensional bar code

④ èrwéimǎ zhīfù
二维码支付 _____
two-dimensional bar code payment

条码技术 9
Bar Code Technology

2. 观看介绍一维条形码和二维码的视频，说一说下列选项哪些是二维码的功能。Watch the video introducing one-dimensional bar codes and two-dimensional bar codes, and talk about which of the following options are the functions of two-dimensional bar codes.

yīwéi tiáoxíngmǎ hé èrwéimǎ de
一维条形码和二维码的
yìngyòng
应用
application of one-dimensional bar codes and two-dimensional bar codes

xìnxī huòqǔ
A. 信息获取
information retrieval

guǎnggào tuīsòng
B. 广告 推送
advertisement push

fāngbiàn gòuwù
C. 方便 购物
convenient shopping

shǒujī zhīfù
D. 手机支付
mobile payment

yōuhuì cùxiāo
E. 优惠促销
special promotions

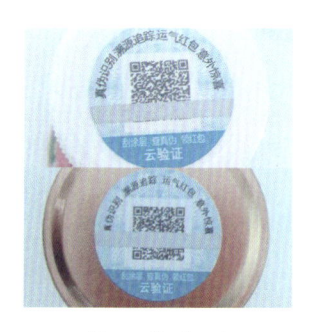

fángwěi sùyuán
F. 防伪 溯源
security traceability

èrwéimǎ de gōngnéng
二维码的功能：_____
functions of two-dimensional bar codes

93

二、课文 kèwén Texts

A 09-01

Yīwéi tiáoxíngmǎ zhǐshì zài shuǐpíng fāngxiàng biǎodá xìnxī, zài chuízhí fāngxiàng bù biǎodá rènhé xìnxī, qí yǒu yídìng de gāodù tōngcháng shì wèile biànyú yuèdúqì duìzhǔn.

一维条形码只是在水平方向表达信息,在垂直方向不表达任何信息,其有一定的高度通常是为了便于阅读器对准。

译文 yìwén Text in English

A one-dimensional bar code expresses information only in horizontal direction and nothing in vertical direction, and it's of certain height, which is usually used to facilitate the alignment of readers.

普通词语 pǔtōng cíyǔ General Vocabulary 09-02

1.	只是	zhǐshì	adv.	only
2.	表达	biǎodá	v.	express
3.	任何	rènhé	pron.	any
4.	其	qí	pron.	he, she, it, they
5.	一定	yídìng	adj.	certain
6.	通常	tōngcháng	adv.	usually
7.	便于	biànyú	v.	be easy to

专业词语 zhuānyè cíyǔ Specialized Vocabulary 09-03

1.	一维条形码（一维码）	yīwéi tiáoxíngmǎ (yīwéimǎ)	n.	one-dimensional bar code
2.	方向	fāngxiàng	n.	direction
3.	高度	gāodù	n.	height
4.	阅读器	yuèdúqì	n.	reader
5.	对准	duìzhǔn	phr.	align

条码技术
Bar Code Technology 9

B 🎧 09-04

Èrwéi tiáoxíngmǎ shì zài shuǐpíng hé chuízhí fāngxiàng de èrwéi kōngjiān dōu néng chǔcún
二维条形码是在水平和垂直方向的二维空间都能储存
xìnxī de tiáoxíngmǎ.
信息的条形码。

译文 yìwén Text in English

A two-dimensional bar code is a bar code that can store information in two-dimensional space in both horizontal and vertical directions.

专业词语 zhuānyè cíyǔ Specialized Vocabulary 🎧 09-05

1. 二维条形码（二维码） èrwéi tiáoxíngmǎ (èrwéimǎ) n. two-dimensional bar code
2. 二维空间 èrwéi kōngjiān phr. two-dimensional space

三、视听说 shì-tīng-shuō Viewing, Listening and Speaking

看视频，进一步了解一维条形码和二维条形码，判断它们分别具有哪些特性。**Watch the video to further understand one-dimensional bar codes and two-dimensional bar codes. Determine what characteristics they have.**

yīwéi tiáoxíngmǎ hé èrwéi tiáoxíngmǎ de
一维条形码和二维条形码的
tèxìng
特性
characteristics of one-dimensional bar codes
and two-dimensional bar codes

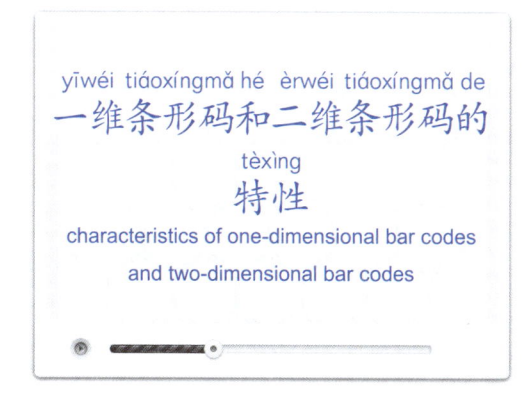

shùjù róngliàng dà
A. 数据容量大
large data capacity

méi yǒu zìmǔ、shùzì xiànzhì
B. 没有字母、数字限制
no restrictions of letters or numbers

róngliàng xiǎo
C. 容量小
small capacity

chǐcùn xiǎo
D. 尺寸小
small dimension

95

      yǒu kàngsǔnhuǐ nénglì   chǐcùn jiào dà

E. 有抗损毁能力   F. 尺寸较大

having anti-damage ability   relatively large dimension

      zhǐ bāohán zìmǔ hé shùzì

G. 只包含字母和数字

containing only letters and numbers

      yīwéi tiáoxíngmǎ de tèxìng

❶ 一维条形码的特性：_____

characteristics of one-dimensional bar codes

      èrwéi tiáoxíngmǎ de tèxìng

❷ 二维条形码的特性：_____

characteristics of two-dimensional bar codes

四、学以致用　xuéyǐzhìyòng　Practicing What You Have Learnt

看视频，了解物流入库时的二维码生成过程，并按生成过程的先后顺序给下列选项排序。**Watch the video to understand the process of two-dimensional code generation when the goods are put in storage, and arrange the following options in order of the process of generation.**

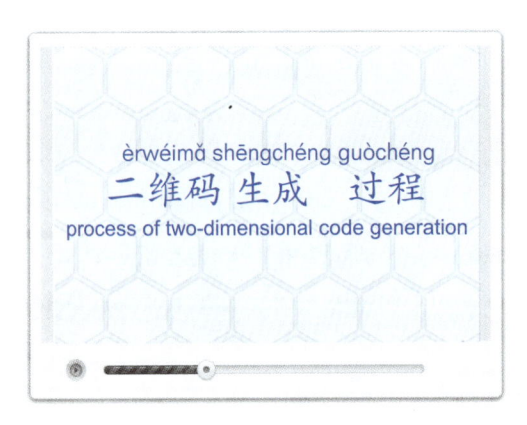

èrwéimǎ shēngchéng guòchéng
二维码 生成 过程
process of two-dimensional code generation

    dǎkāi èrwéimǎ shēngchéngqì   tiāoxuǎn xíngzhuàng、yánsè děng   diǎnjī wánchéng

A. 打开二维码生成器   B. 挑选 形状、颜色等   C. 点击完成

open the two-dimensional   choose the shape, color, etc.   click completed

code generator

    shūrù huòpǐn rù kù xìnxī、shāngpǐn jīběn xìnxī，bāokuò shāngpǐn míngchēng、jiàgé、chǎngjiā、túpiàn děng

D. 输入货品入库信息、商品基本信息，包括商品名称、价格、厂家、图片等

input the warehouse entry information and the basic information of the commodity, including the commodity name, price, manufacturer, picture, etc.

五、小知识　xiǎo zhīshi　Tips

Shāngpǐn de "shēnfènzhèng"
商品 的"身份证"

Shāngpǐn tiáomǎ shì shāngpǐn zài quánqiú liútōng de wéiyī "shēnfènzhèng" hé guójì tōngyòng de
商品 条码是 商品 在全球 流通的唯一"身份证"和国际通用 的
shāngwù yǔyán. Tiáoxíngmǎ 1~3 wèi dàibiǎo bù tóng de guójiā: Zhōngguó (bù hán Gǎng-Ào-Tái)
商务语言。条形码 1～3 位代表不同的国家：中国（不含 港澳台）
shì 690~695, Měiguó shì 000~019、030~039、060~139. Nǐ zhīdào
是 690～695，美国是 000～019、030～039、060～139。你知道
nǐmen guójiā de tiáoxíngmǎ 1~3 wèi shì shénme shùzì ma?
你们国家的条形码 1～3 位是 什么数字吗？

"ID Card" of Commodities

The commodity bar code is the only "ID card" in the global circulation of the products and an internationally accepted business language. The 1-3 digits of the bar code stand for different countries: 690-695 is for China (excluding Hong Kong SAR, Macao SAR and Taiwan province), 000-019, 030-039, and 060-139 are for the United States. Do you know what the first 3 digits of your country's bar code are?

第二部分　Part 2
汉字　Chinese Characters

一、汉字知识　Hànzì zhīshi　Knowledge about Chinese Characters

1. 汉字的笔画（9）Strokes of Chinese characters (9)

笔画 Strokes	名称 Names	例字 Examples
㇗	横折折撇 héngzhézhépiě	延、建
㇗	竖折撇 shùzhépiě	专

2. 汉字的结构（5）Structures of Chinese characters (5)

结构类型 Structure types	例字 Examples	结构图示 Illustrations
全包围结构 Fully-enclosed structure	国	□

（续表）

结构类型 Structure types	例字 Examples	结构图示 Illustrations
半包围结构 Semi-enclosed structure	医 边 问 唐 凶	▢ ▢ ▢ ▢ ▢

二、汉字认读与书写　Hànzì rèndú yǔ shūxiě　**The Recognition and Writing of Chinese Characters**

认读下列词语，并试着读写构成词语的汉字。**Recognize the following words, and try to read and write the Chinese characters forming these words.**

二维条形码　　水平　　方向　　垂直

二		维		条		形	
码		水		平		方	
向		垂		直			

第三部分　Part 3　日常用语 Daily Expressions

① 我该怎么办？ Wǒ gāi zěnme bàn? What shall I do?

② 麻烦你告诉我他的电话号码。Máfan nǐ gàosu wǒ tā de diànhuà hàomǎ. Excuse me, could you please tell me his phone number?

③ 真不好意思，我忘了给你打电话。Zhēn bù hǎoyìsi, wǒ wàngle gěi nǐ dǎ diànhuà. Sorry, I forgot to phone you.

第四部分　Part 4　单元实训 Unit Practical Training

条形码技术应用实训　tiáoxíngmǎ jìshù yìngyòng shíxùn
Practical Training of Bar Code Technology Application

实训目的 Training purpose

通过本次实训，了解一维条形码和二维条形码的应用。

Through this practical training, understand the application of one-dimensional bar codes and two-dimensional bar codes.

实训组织 Training organization

每组 4 人。

Each group consists of 4 trainees.

实训步骤 Training steps

❶ 教师展示常见的一维条形码（13 位）、二维条形码。

The teacher illustrates common one-dimensional bar codes (13 digits) and two-dimensional bar codes.

❷ 将参加实训的人员分成若干组，每组内 2 名组员负责收集日常商品中的一维条形码照片 5 张（如教材、饮料瓶上的条形码等），另 2 名组员负责收集二维条形码的应用场景 5 个（如高铁车票上的二维条形码、微信二维条形码名片等）。

Divide the trainees into groups. Two members of each group collect 5 photos of one-dimensional bar codes on daily commodities (such as bar codes on textbooks, beverage bottles, etc.), and the other two members collect 5 application scenarios using two-dimensional bar codes (such as two-dimensional bar codes on high-speed rail tickets, WeChat business cards with two-dimensional bar codes, etc.).

❸ 各组分别说一说一维条形码、二维条形码的用途和特征。

Each group talks about the uses and characteristics of one-dimensional bar codes and two-dimensional bar codes.

❺ 教师总结评价，实训结束。

The teacher summarizes and evaluates, and the training ends.

第五部分　Part 5　单元小结 Unit Summary

cíyǔ 词语 Vocabulary

普通词语　General Vocabulary

1.	只是	zhǐshì	adv.	only
2.	表达	biǎodá	v.	express
3.	任何	rènhé	pron.	any
4.	其	qí	pron.	he, she, it, they
5.	一定	yídìng	adj.	certain
6.	通常	tōngcháng	adv.	usually
7.	便于	biànyú	v.	be easy to

专业词语　Specialized Vocabulary

1.	一维条形码（一维码）	yīwéi tiáoxíngmǎ (yīwéimǎ)	n.	one-dimensional bar code
2.	方向	fāngxiàng	n.	direction

词语 cíyǔ Vocabulary

3.	高度	gāodù	n.	height
4.	阅读器	yuèdúqì	n.	reader
5.	对准	duìzhǔn	phr.	align
6.	二维条形码（二维码）	èrwéi tiáoxíngmǎ (èrwéimǎ)	n.	two-dimensional bar code
7.	二维空间	èrwéi kōngjiān	phr.	two-dimensional space

补充专业词语　Supplementary Specialized Vocabulary

1.	防伪溯源	fángwěi sùyuán	phr.	security traceability
2.	优惠促销	yōuhuì cùxiāo	phr.	special promotion
3.	广告推送	guǎnggào tuīsòng	phr.	advertisement push
4.	手机支付	shǒujī zhīfù	phr.	mobile payment
5.	信息获取	xìnxī huòqǔ	phr.	information retrieval
6.	抗损毁能力	kàngsǔnhuǐ nénglì	phr.	anti-damage ability

句子 jùzi Sentences

1. 一维条形码只是在水平方向表达信息。
2. 二维条形码是在水平和垂直方向的二维空间都能储存信息的条形码。
3. 一维条形码数据容量较小，30个字符左右，只能包含字母和数字，尺寸较大，条形码损坏后就不能读取信息了。
4. 二维条形码数据容量更大，没有字母、数字的限制，尺寸小，具有抗损毁能力。

10

Quánqiú Dìngwèi Xìtǒng （GPS）
全球定位系统（GPS）
Global Positioning System (GPS)

GPS de gòuchéng
GPS 的 构成
the components of GPS

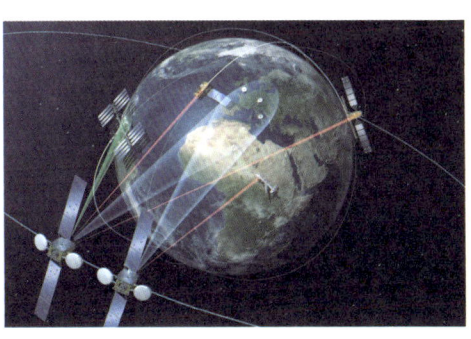

kōngjiān bùfen　　GPS wèixīng xīngzuò
空间 部分 — GPS 卫星 星座
space segment–GPS satellite constellation

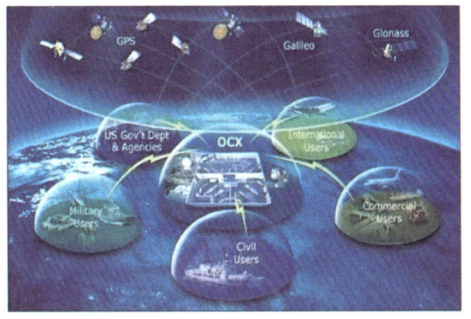

dìmiàn kòngzhì bùfen　　dìmiàn jiānkòng xìtǒng
地面 控制 部分 — 地面 监控 系统
control segment–ground monitoring system

yònghù bùfen　　GPS xìnhào jiēshōujī
用户 部分 — GPS 信号 接收机
user segment–GPS signal receiver

101

题解　Introduction

1. 学习内容：全球定位系统的构成、作用、特点、工作原理及应用。
   Learning content: The composition, function, characteristics, working principles and application of the Global Positioning System (GPS).

2. 知识目标：掌握与全球定位系统相关的核心词语及表达，复习汉字的笔画、笔顺和结构，学写相关汉字。
   Knowledge objectives: Grasp the core vocabulary and expressions related to the Global Positioning System (GPS), review strokes, stroke orders and structures of Chinese characters, and learn to write the related Chinese characters.

3. 技能目标：能在生活中实际运用全球定位系统。
   Skill objective: Be able to use the Global Positioning System (GPS) in life.

第一部分　Part 1

课文　Texts

一、热身　rèshēn　Warm-up

1. 给词语选择对应的图片。**Choose the corresponding pictures for the words.**

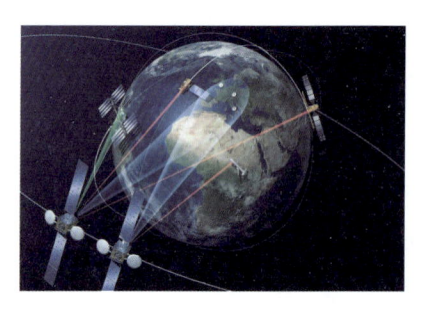

A.

B.

C.

❶ chē zài GPS
   车载 GPS ＿＿＿＿＿＿
   vehicle GPS

❷ shǒujī GPS
   手机 GPS ＿＿＿＿＿＿
   mobile phone GPS

❸ Quánqiú Dìngwèi Xìtǒng
   全球 定位 系统 ＿＿＿＿＿＿
   Global Positioning System

102

全球定位系统（GPS）
Global Positioning System (GPS)

2. 看视频，了解GPS的构成，并将下列选项填入图片中的相应位置。**Watch the video to understand the composition of the Global Positioning System (GPS) and fill the following options in the corresponding positions in the picture.**

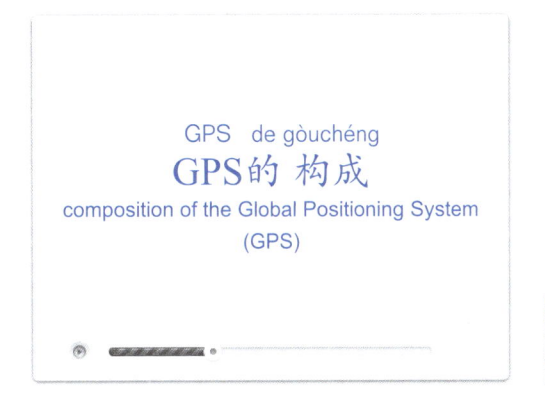

<GPS de gòuchéng>
GPS的 构成
composition of the Global Positioning System (GPS)

GPS 的组成

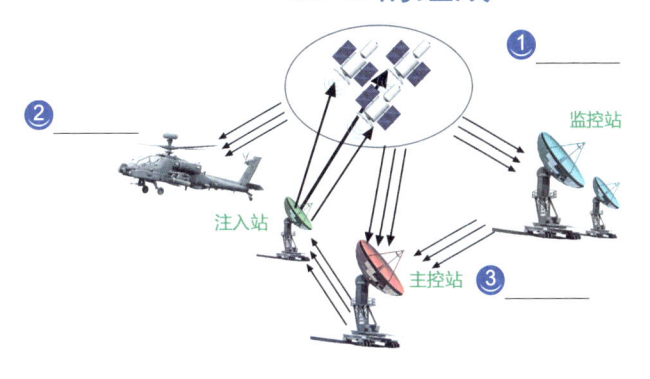

① _____
② _____
③ _____

监控站
注入站
主控站

kōngjiān bùfen
A. 空间 部分
space segment

dìmiàn jiānkòng bùfen
B. 地面 监控 部分
control segment

yònghù bùfen
C. 用户 部分
user segment

二、课文　kèwén　Texts

A 🎧 10-01

　　GPS néng wèi yònghù tígōng quánfāngwèi dǎoháng hé dìngwèi fúwù,　jùyǒu gāo jīngdù、
　　GPS 能 为 用户 提供 全方位 导航 和 定位 服务，具有 高精度、
quántiānhòu、gāo xiàolǜ、duō gōngnéng、cāozuò jiǎnbiàn、yìngyòng guǎngfàn děng tèdiǎn.
全天候、高效率、 多 功能、操作 简便、应用 广泛 等 特点。

译文 yìwén Text in English

　　The GPS can produce all-round navigation and positioning services for users, with characteristics of high precision, all-weather service, high efficiency, multi-function, ease of operation, wide range of applications and so on.

103

中文＋物流管理（中级）

普通词语 pǔtōng cíyǔ General Vocabulary 🎧 10-02

1.	能	néng	aux.	can
2.	提供	tígōng	v.	provide
3.	简便	jiǎnbiàn	adj.	simple and convenient
4.	应用	yìngyòng	v.	use, employ, apply
5.	广泛	guǎngfàn	adj.	wide, broad
6.	特点	tèdiǎn	n.	characteristic

专业词语 zhuānyè cíyǔ Specialized Vocabulary 🎧 10-03

1.	全方位	quánfāngwèi	n.	(in) all directions/dimensions
2.	精度	jīngdù	n.	precision, accuracy
3.	全天候	quántiānhòu	adj.	all-weather

B 🎧 10-04

GPS jiēshōujī néng jìlù bù tóng wèixīng fāchū de xìnhào dàodá jiēshōujī de shíjiān,
GPS 接收机能记录不同卫星发出的信号到达接收机的时间，

lìyòng gāi shíjiān yǔ wèixīng fāshè xìnhào de shíjiān jiù kěyǐ jìsuàn jiēshōujī yǔ zhè jǐ kē wèixīng
利用该时间与卫星发射信号的时间就可以计算接收机与这几颗卫星

zhījiān de jùlí. Yóuyú wèixīng de wèizhì yǐ zhī, yīncǐ tōngguò jìsuàn jiù kěyǐ zhīdào jiēshōujī
之间的距离。由于卫星的位置已知，因此通过计算就可以知道接收机

suǒ zài de jīngdù, wěidù hé gāodù.
所在的经度、纬度和高度。

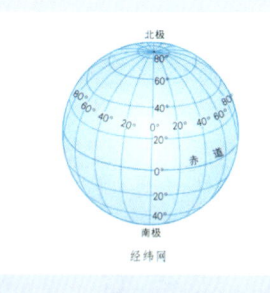

译文 yìwén Text in English

The GPS receiver can record the time when the signals sent by different satellites arrive at the receiver, and the distance between the receiver and these satellites can be calculated with this time and the time when the signals are transmitted by the satellites. Since the positions of the satellites are known, the longitude, latitude and altitude of the receiver can be known through calculation.

104

普通词语 pǔtōng cíyǔ General Vocabulary 🎧 10-05

1.	到达	dàodá	v.	arrive
2.	该	gāi	pron.	this, that
3.	与	yǔ	conj.	and, together with
4.	计算	jìsuàn	v.	calculate
5.	颗	kē	m.	*used of grains and grain-like things*
6.	位置	wèizhì	n.	position
7.	知	zhī	v.	know
8.	因此	yīncǐ	conj.	so, therefore
9.	通过	tōngguò	prep.	through, by
10.	在	zài	v.	*indicating where a person or thing is*

专业词语 zhuānyè cíyǔ Specialized Vocabulary 🎧 10-06

1.	接收机	jiēshōujī	n.	receiver
2.	卫星	wèixīng	n.	satellite
3.	信号	xìnhào	n.	signal
4.	发射	fāshè	v.	transmit, emit
5.	经度	jīngdù	n.	longitude
6.	纬度	wěidù	n.	latitude

三、视听说 shì-tīng-shuō Viewing, Listening and Speaking

看视频，了解GPS的应用，判断下列图片分别属于哪些应用领域，并说说这些应用的好处。**Watch the video to understand the application of GPS. Determine which application fields the following pictures belong to respectively, and talk about the benefits of these application.**

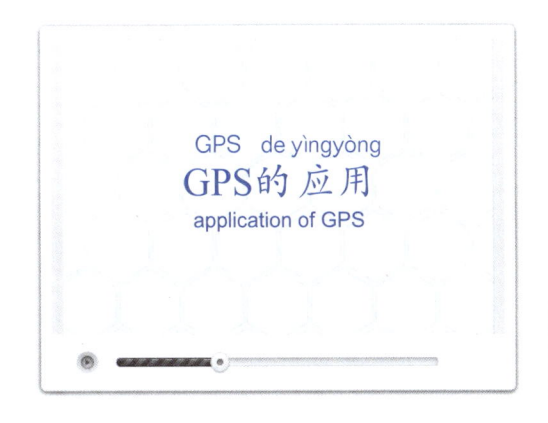

GPS de yìngyòng
GPS的应用
application of GPS

中文 + 物流管理（中级）

A.

B.

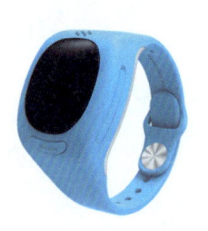

C.

D.

① chēliàng dìngwèi
车辆 定位 _____
vehicle positioning

② GPS dǎoháng
GPS 导航 _____
GPS navigation

③ chǒngwù gēnzōng
宠物 跟踪 _____
pet tracking

④ rénwù dìngwèi
人物 定位 _____
figure positioning

四、学以致用　xuéyǐzhìyòng　Practicing What You Have Learnt

看视频，学习如何使用手机 GPS，并按照使用流程的先后顺序给下列选项排序。**Watch the video to learn how to use mobile phone GPS and arrange the following options in order of the usage process.**

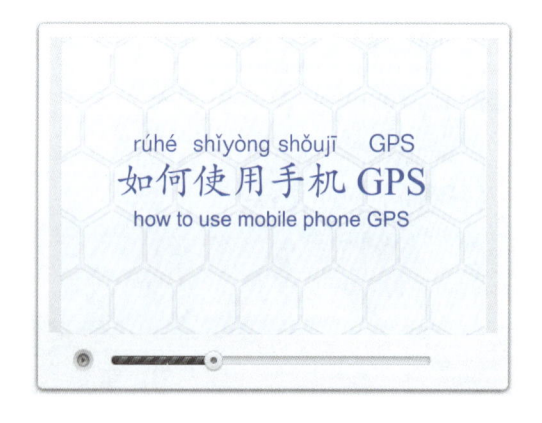

rúhé shǐyòng shǒujī GPS
如何使用手机 GPS
how to use mobile phone GPS

全球定位系统（GPS） 10
Global Positioning System (GPS)

A. dǎkāi dìtú, shūrù qǐdiǎn hé zhōngdiǎn
打开地图，输入起点和 终点
open the map, and input the starting point and end point

B. dǎkāi shǒujī GPS
打开手机 GPS
open mobile phone GPS

C. kāishǐ dǎoháng
开始 导航
start the navigation

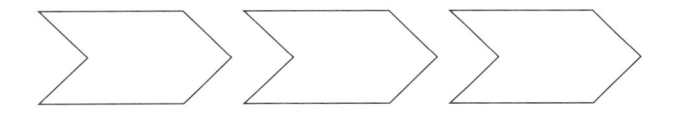

五、小知识 xiǎo zhīshi Tips

GPS shǐyòng zhùyì shìxiàng
GPS 使用注意事项

GPS shèbèi yīng cúnfàng zài gānzào、tōngfēng、yīnliáng de huánjìng zhōng, yǐ fángzhǐ cháng
GPS设备应 存放在干燥、通风、阴凉的环境 中，以防止长

shíjiān bú yòng bèi fǔshí, cóng'ér yǐngxiǎng GPS de dìngwèi jīngdù hé shǐyòng shòumìng.
时间不用 被腐蚀，从而 影响 GPS 的定位精度和使用 寿命。

Dǎléi shí yīng jíshí guānbì yíqì, tíngzhǐ shǐyòng, fángzhǐ yíqì sǔnhuài.
打雷时应 及时关闭仪器，停止 使用，防止仪器损坏。

zài shǐyòng GPS jiēshōujī de guòchéng zhōng, yào qīng ná qīng fàng, bìmiǎn kēpèng,
在 使用GPS 接收机的 过程 中，要轻拿轻放，避免磕碰，

quèbǎo yíqì shǐyòng ānquán.
确保仪器使用 安全。

107

> **Notes for Using GPS**
>
> GPS devices should be kept in a dry, ventilated and cool environment to prevent corrosion resulting from lying idle for a long time, thus affecting the positioning accuracy and service life of GPS.
>
> When it thunders, turn off the instrument in time, and stop using it to prevent the instrument from being damaged.
>
> In the course of using the GPS receiver, try to handle it gently to avoid collision and ensure the safety.

第二部分 Part 2
汉字 Chinese Characters

一、汉字知识 Hànzì zhīshi Knowledge about Chinese Characters

1. 汉字的笔画（总表） Strokes of Chinese characters (general table)

一	丨	丿	丶	丶	𠃌	㇄
㇀	⼇	亅	丿	㇏	⼃	⼁
𠃍	⼂	⺄	⺄	𠃌	⼄	⺄
⻊	⼂	⼁	⼂	⼂	⼂	⼂

2. 汉字的笔顺（总表） Stroke orders of Chinese characters (general table)

笔顺规则 Rules of stroke orders	例字 Examples
先横后竖	十
先撇后捺	人、八
先上后下	三
先左后右	人
先中间后两边	小
先外边后里边	问
先外后里再封口	国、日

3. 汉字的结构（总表） Structures of Chinese characters (general table)

类型 Structure types	结构图示 Illustrations	例字 Examples
独体结构	□	生、不
品字形结构	⊞	品
上下结构	⊟ ⊟	爸、节

（续表）

类型 Structure types	结构图示 Illustrations	例字 Examples
上中下结构	三	意
左右结构	⊞	银、饭
左中右结构	⊞	班、微
全包围结构	▢	国
半包围结构	⊓ ⊔ ⊐ ⊏ ⊒	医、边、问、唐、凶

二、汉字认读与书写　Hànzì rèndú yǔ shūxiě　The Recognition and Writing of Chinese Characters

认读下列词语，并试着读写构成词语的汉字。Recognize the following words, and try to read and write the Chinese characters forming these words.

导航　　定位　　信号　　精度

| 导 | | | 航 | | | 定 | | | 位 | | |
| 信 | | | 号 | | | 精 | | | 度 | | |

第三部分　Part 3
日常用语　Daily Expressions

❶ 谢谢你的礼物，我很喜欢。Xièxie nǐ de lǐwù, wǒ hěn xǐhuan. Thanks for your gift. I like it very much.
❷ 谢谢您的邀请，我一定去。Xièxie nín de yāoqǐng, wǒ yídìng qù. Thanks for your invitation. I promise I will be there.
❸ 我该走了，再见。Wǒ gāi zǒu le, zàijiàn. I've got to go. Bye.

第四部分　Part 4
单元实训　Unit Practical Training

GPS 应用实训　GPS yìngyòng shíxùn
Practical Training of GPS Application

实训目的 Training purpose
通过本次实训，了解 GPS 的应用。
Through this practical training, understand the application of GPS.

实训组织 Training organization
每组 4 人。
Each group consists of 4 trainees.

实训步骤 Training steps

❶ 打开手机定位功能，在地图上找到自己的位置。
Turn on the mobile positioning function and find your position in a map.

❷ 选择一个目的地（如火车站），在地图上查询距离，并说出驾车前往目的地的路线有几种选择。
Choose a destination (such as a railway station), look up the distance in the map and tell how many routes there are to drive to the destination.

❸ 小组讨论说出 2 个日常生活中使用 GPS 导航或定位功能的案例。
Each group discusses and tells two cases where navigation or positioning functions of GPS are used in daily life.

❹ 教师总结评价，实训结束。
The teacher summarizes and evaluates, and the training ends.

第五部分　Part 5　单元小结 Unit Summary

cíyǔ 词语 Vocabulary

普通词语　General Vocabulary

1.	能	néng	aux.	can
2.	提供	tígōng	v.	provide
3.	简便	jiǎnbiàn	adj.	simple and convenient
4.	应用	yìngyòng	v.	use, employ, apply
5.	广泛	guǎngfàn	adj.	wide, broad
6.	特点	tèdiǎn	n.	characteristic
7.	到达	dàodá	v.	arrive
8.	该	gāi	pron.	this, that
9.	与	yǔ	conj.	and, together with
10.	计算	jìsuàn	v.	calculate
11.	颗	kē	m.	used of grains and grain-like things
12.	位置	wèizhì	n.	position
13.	知	zhī	v.	know
14.	因此	yīncǐ	conj.	so, therefore
15.	通过	tōngguò	prep.	through, by
16.	在	zài	v.	indicating where a person or thing is

专业词语　Specialized Vocabulary

1.	全方位	quánfāngwèi	n.	(in) all directions/dimensions
2.	精度	jīngdù	n.	precision, accuracy

110

全球定位系统（GPS）
Global Positioning System (GPS)

cíyǔ 词语 Vocabulary

3.	全天候	quántiānhòu	adj.	all-weather
4.	接收机	jiēshōujī	n.	receiver
5.	卫星	wèixīng	n.	satellite
6.	信号	xìnhào	n.	signal
7.	发射	fāshè	v.	transmit, emit
8.	经度	jīngdù	n.	longitude
9.	纬度	wěidù	n.	latitude

补充专业词语　Supplementary Specialized Vocabulary

1.	主控站	zhǔkòngzhàn	n.	main control station
2.	监控站	jiānkòngzhàn	n.	monitor station
3.	注入站	zhùrùzhàn	n.	upload station
4.	卫星星座	wèixīng xīngzuò	phr.	satellite constellation

jùzi 句子 Sentences

1. GPS 能为用户提供全方位导航和定位服务。
2. GPS 具有高精度、全天候、高效率、多功能、操作简便、应用广泛等特点。
3. GPS 主要包括三大部分：空间部分、地面控制部分和用户部分。
4. GPS 的应用领域无所不在。

附录 Appendixes

词语总表　Vocabulary

序号	生词	拼音	词性	词义	普通G/专业S	所属单元
1	安全行驶报警系统	ānquán xíngshǐ bàojǐng xìtǒng	phr.	safe driving alarm system	S	8B
2	安装	ānzhuāng	v.	install	G	8B
3	包含	bāohán	v.	contain	G	1A
4	保管区	bǎoguǎnqū	n.	storage area	S	5A
5	报警	bào//jǐng	v.	report (a danger, etc.) to the police or public authorities, give an alarm	S	8B
6	比较	bǐjiào	adv.	comparatively, relatively	G	4B
7	便于	biànyú	v.	be easy to	G	9A
8	标签	biāoqiān	n.	label	S	2A
9	表达	biǎodá	v.	express	G	9A
10	并	bìng	conj.	and	G	4A
11	波动	bōdòng	v.	fluctuate	S	3
12	播种	bō//zhǒng	v.	grow/cultivate by sowing seeds	S	4A
13	播种式拣选	bōzhǒngshì jiǎnxuǎn	phr.	DAS picking	S	4A
14	补充	bǔchōng	v.	replenish, supplement	G	2A
15	补货	bǔ huò	phr.	replenish goods	S	5A
16	部门	bùmén	n.	department	S	1A
17	采购	cǎigòu	v.	purchase	S	1A
18	采用	cǎiyòng	v.	use, adopt	G	6A
19	操作	cāozuò	v.	operate	G	3B
20	测量	cèliáng	v.	measure	G	10B
21	层	céng	m.	layer, tier	G	5A
22	查询	cháxún	v.	inquiry	S	1B
23	长	cháng	adj.	long	G	3B
24	超速	chāosù	v.	exceed the speed limit	G	8B
25	超重	chāo//zhòng	v.	overload	S	6B
26	朝	cháo	v.	face	G	6B
27	车辆管理系统	chēliàng guǎnlǐ xìtǒng	phr.	vehicle management system	S	8A
28	衬垫	chèn diàn	phr.	pad	S	6B
29	成	chéng	v.	amount to (a considerable number/amount)	G	4A

（续表）

序号	生词	拼音	词性	词义	普通 G/专业 S	所属单元
30	成为	chéngwéi	v.	become	G	2B
31	承运商	chéngyùnshāng	n.	carrier	S	8A
32	充分	chōngfèn	adj.	full, abundant	G	6A
33	重合度	chónghédù	n.	overlap ratio	S	4B
34	出来	chūlái	v.	used after certain verbs to indicate movement from inside out (towards the speaker)	G	4A
35	处理	chǔlǐ	v.	handle, deal with	G	1B
36	储位	chǔwèi	n.	storage location	S	3A
37	次	cì	m.	time	G	3A
38	次品	cìpǐn	n.	defective product, defective goods	S	7B
39	从	cóng	prep.	from	G	1B
40	存货	cúnhuò	n.	inventory	S	1B
41	存货档案	cúnhuò dàng'àn	phr.	inventory file	S	5
42	存货分配	cúnhuò fēnpèi	phr.	inventory allocation	S	1
43	存量	cúnliàng	n.	stock	S	5B
44	存在	cúnzài	v.	exist	G	7A
45	搭配	dāpèi	v.	arrange according to given requirements, organize in pairs/groups	S	2
46	搭配销售	dāpèi xiāoshòu	phr.	tie-in sale	S	2
47	大	dà	adj.	big	G	3B
48	代表	dàibiǎo	v.	represent, stand for	G	1A
49	单个	dāngè	adj.	single	G	3B
50	单价	dānjià	n.	unit price	S	1A
51	单据	dānjù	n.	receipt, voucher	S	1B
52	但	dàn	conj.	but, yet, still	G	3B
53	当	dāng	prep.	(just) at (a time/place)	G	5B
54	导航	dǎoháng	v.	navigate	S	8B
55	导航仪	dǎohángyí	n.	navigator	S	8B
56	到	dào	v.	up until/to, by	G	1B
57	到	dào	v.	used as a complement of a verb indicating the result of an action	G	1B
58	到达	dàodá	v.	arrive	G	10B
59	低	dī	adj.	low, below the average	G	5B
60	电子标签拣选系统	diànzǐ biāoqiān jiǎnxuǎn xìtǒng	phr.	digital picking system	S	3

（续表）

序号	生词	拼音	词性	词义	普通G/专业S	所属单元
61	电子订货	diànzǐ dìnghuò	phr.	electronic ordering	S	1
62	调度	diàodù	v.	manage, dispatch	S	8
63	调度员	diàodùyuán	n.	dispatcher	S	8
64	订单量	dìngdānliàng	n.	order quantity	S	3B
65	订购	dìnggòu	v.	order	S	1A
66	订货	dìng//huò	v.	order goods	S	1A
67	订货周期	dìnghuò zhōuqī	phr.	ordering cycle	S	1
68	动作	dòngzuò	n.	action, movement	G	3B
69	对	duì	prep.	concerning, regarding	G	2A
70	对准	duìzhǔn	phr.	align	S	9A
71	多	duō	adj.	many, much, more	G	3B
72	二维空间	èrwéi kōngjiān	phr.	two-dimensional space	S	9B
73	二维条形码（二维码）	èrwéi tiáoxíngmǎ (èrwéimǎ)	n.	two-dimensional bar code	S	9B
74	发出	fāchū	v.	issued by	G	1A
75	发票	fāpiào	n.	invoice	S	7
76	发射	fāshè	v.	transmit, emit	S	10B
77	发送	fāsòng	v.	send	G	8A
78	方法	fāngfǎ	n.	method	G	4A
79	方向	fāngxiàng	n.	direction	S	9A
80	防伪溯源	fángwěi sùyuán	phr.	security traceability	S	9
81	防止	fángzhǐ	v.	prevent	G	6B
82	分	fēn	v.	divide, split	G	5A
83	分割	fēngē	v.	cut apart, separate	S	2A
84	分货	fēn huò	phr.	sort goods	S	4A
85	分拣	fēnjiǎn	v.	sort	S	2A
86	分选加工	fēn xuǎn jiāgōng	phr.	sorting processing	S	2B
87	分装加工	fēn zhuāng jiāgōng	phr.	packaging processing	S	2B
88	服务	fúwù	n.	service	G	1B
89	辅助	fǔzhù	v.	assist	G	2A
90	复杂	fùzá	adj.	complex	G	2A
91	该	gāi	pron.	this, that	G	10B
92	高	gāo	adj.	high	G	4B
93	高度	gāodù	n.	height	S	9A

（续表）

序号	生词	拼音	词性	词义	普通G/专业S	所属单元
94	各	gè	pron.	all, every	G	3A
95	各个	gègè	pron.	each, every	G	3A
96	工具	gōngjù	n.	tool	G	6A
97	供应商	gōngyìngshāng	n.	supplier	S	1A
98	广泛	guǎngfàn	adj.	wide, broad	G	10A
99	广告推送	guǎnggào tuīsòng	phr.	advertisement push	S	9
100	轨迹	guǐjì	n.	trajectory	G	8A
101	过期	guò//qī	v.	expire	S	7B
102	耗时	hàoshí	v.	consume time	G	3B
103	合理	hélǐ	adj.	reasonable	G	6A
104	后	hòu	n.	(of time) (in) future	G	2B
105	回复	huífù	v.	reply	G	8A
106	活动	huódòng	n.	activity	G	7A
107	或者	huòzhě	conj.	or	G	7A
108	计量	jìliàng	v.	measure	S	2A
109	计算	jìsuàn	v.	calculate	G	10B
110	记录	jìlù	v.	record	S	8B
111	驾驶	jiàshǐ	v.	drive	G	8B
112	监控	jiānkòng	v.	monitor	G	8A
113	监控站	jiānkòngzhàn	n.	monitor station	S	10
114	拣货量	jiǎnhuòliàng	n.	picking volume	S	4B
115	拣货区	jiǎnhuòqū	n.	picking area	S	5A
116	拣选	jiǎnxuǎn	v.	pick, select	S	3A
117	简便	jiǎnbiàn	adj.	simple and convenient	G	10A
118	简单	jiǎndān	adj.	simple	G	2A
119	降低货损	jiàngdī huòsǔn	phr.	reduce cargo damage	S	4
120	较	jiào	adv.	comparatively, relatively	G	3B
121	阶段	jiēduàn	n.	stage, phase	G	1B
122	接到	jiēdào	phr.	receive	G	1B
123	接收机	jiēshōujī	n.	receiver	S	10B
124	节省人力	jiéshěng rénlì	phr.	save manpower	S	4
125	结算方式	jiésuàn fāngshì	phr.	settlement method	S	1A
126	尽量	jǐnliàng	adv.	as far as possible	G	6A

（续表）

序号	生词	拼音	词性	词义	普通G/专业S	所属单元
127	进行	jìnxíng	v.	carry out	G	2A
128	禁止	jìnzhǐ	v.	prohibit, forbid	G	6B
129	经度	jīngdù	n.	longitude	S	10B
130	经过	jīngguò	v.	(of action, etc.) go through	G	2B
131	精度	jīngdù	n.	precision, accuracy	S	10A
132	精制加工	jīngzhì jiāgōng	phr.	refining processing	S	2B
133	净菜	jìngcài	n.	clean vegetable	G	2B
134	具有	jùyǒu	v.	have, possess	G	8B
135	距离	jùlí	n.	distance	S	3B
136	看	kàn	v.	depend on	G	5B
137	抗损毁能力	kàngsǔnhuǐ nénglì	phr.	anti-damage ability	S	9
138	颗	kē	m.	*used of grains and grain-like things*	G	10B
139	客户档案	kèhù dàng'àn	phr.	customer file	S	1
140	快	kuài	adj.	quick, fast	G	3B
141	冷冻加工	lěngdòng jiāgōng	phr.	freezing processing	S	2B
142	利弊	lìbì	n.	pros and cons, advantages and disadvantages	S	3
143	利用	lìyòng	v.	make use of, utilize	G	6A
144	辆	liàng	m.	*used with vehicles*	G	8A
145	流通加工	liútōng jiāgōng	phr.	distribution processing	S	2A
146	慢	màn	adj.	slow	G	4B
147	每	měi	pron.	each	G	3A
148	难度	nándù	n.	difficulty	G	4B
149	能	néng	aux.	can	G	10A
150	配送	pèisòng	v.	distribute, deliver	S	6B
151	配装	pèi zhuāng	phr.	load	S	6A
152	烹调	pēngtiáo	v.	cook	G	2B
153	批	pī	m.	batch	G	4A
154	批次	pīcì	m.	batch	S	6A
155	批量	pīliàng	n.	size/volume of a batch (of products)	S	6A
156	疲劳	píláo	adj.	tired, fatigued	G	8B
157	品种	pǐnzhǒng	n.	breed, variety	S	3B
158	平衡	pínghéng	adj.	balanced	G	6B
159	凭据	píngjù	n.	evidence, proof	S	1A

(续表)

序号	生词	拼音	词性	词义	普通G/专业S	所属单元
160	其	qí	pron.	he, she, it, they	G	9A
161	企业	qǐyè	n.	enterprise	S	1A
162	轻	qīng	adj.	light, of little weight	G	6B
163	情况	qíngkuàng	n.	situation	G	3B
164	取	qǔ	v.	get, collect	G	3A
165	全方位	quánfāngwèi	n.	(in) all directions/dimensions	S	10A
166	全天候	quántiānhòu	adj.	all-weather	S	10A
167	确认	quèrèn	v.	confirm	S	1B
168	任何	rènhé	pron.	any	G	9A
169	容积率	róngjīlǜ	n.	volume ratio	S	6A
170	商品	shāngpǐn	n.	commodity	S	1A
171	上	shàng	n.	upper position	G	5A
172	少	shǎo	adj.	few, little	G	3B
173	设定订单号	shèdìng dìngdānhào	phr.	set an order number	S	1
174	涉及	shèjí	v.	involve	G	1B
175	生产加工	shēngchǎn jiāgōng	phr.	production processing	S	2A
176	生产领域	shēngchǎn lǐngyù	phr.	production field	S	2
177	生鲜	shēngxiān	n.	raw and fresh	G	2B
178	时候	shíhou	n.	(the duration of) time	G	6A
179	食品	shípǐn	n.	food	G	2B
180	食用	shíyòng	v.	eat	G	2B
181	适用	shìyòng	adj.	suitable, applicable	G	3B
182	收据	shōujù	n.	receipt	S	7
183	手机支付	shǒujī zhīfù	phr.	mobile payment	S	9
184	蔬菜	shūcài	n.	vegetable	G	2B
185	数据存储	shùjù cúnchǔ	phr.	data storage	S	4
186	拴标签	shuān biāoqiān	phr.	label	S	2A
187	损坏	sǔnhuài	v.	damage, break	G	6B
188	所以	suǒyǐ	conj.	so, therefore	G	3B
189	它	tā	pron.	it	G	1A
190	特点	tèdiǎn	n.	characteristic	G	10A
191	提供	tígōng	v.	provide	G	10A
192	提前	tíqián	v.	do (sth.) in advance / ahead of time	G	8A

（续表）

序号	生词	拼音	词性	词义	普通 G/专业 S	所属单元
193	提醒	tí//xǐng	v.	remind	G	8A
194	体积	tǐjī	n.	volume, size	S	6
195	贴标志	tiē biāozhì	phr.	paste marks	S	2A
196	通常	tōngcháng	adv.	usually	G	9A
197	通过	tōngguò	prep.	through, by	G	10B
198	同一	tóngyī	adj.	(one and the) same, identical	G	6A
199	退回	tuìhuí	v.	return, send back	G	7A
200	退货	tuì//huò	v.	return goods	S	7A
201	托盘补货	tuōpán bǔ huò	phr.	pallet replenishment	S	5
202	外	wài	n.	the outside	G	6B
203	为	wéi	v.	become, turn/change into	G	5A
204	纬度	wěidù	n.	latitude	S	10B
205	卫星	wèixīng	n.	satellite	S	10B
206	卫星星座	wèixīng xīngzuò	phr.	satellite constellation	S	10
207	为了	wèile	prep.	for, in order to	G	6A
208	位置	wèizhì	n.	position	G	10B
209	问题	wèntí	n.	problem, question	G	7B
210	系统	xìtǒng	n.	system	S	8A
211	下	xià	n.	lower position	G	5A
212	相同	xiāngtóng	adj.	same	G	4A
213	响应速度	xiǎngyìng sùdù	phr.	response speed	S	3B
214	向	xiàng	prep.	*indicating target of action*	G	1A
215	项	xiàng	m.	*used of itemized things*	G	7A
216	消费领域	xiāofèi lǐngyù	phr.	consumption field	S	2
217	小	xiǎo	adj.	small	G	6A
218	新鲜	xīnxiān	adj.	fresh	G	2B
219	信号	xìnhào	n.	signal	S	10B
220	信息获取	xìnxī huòqǔ	phr.	information retrieval	S	9
221	行车记录仪	xíngchē jìlùyí	phr.	dashcam	S	8B
222	行驶	xíngshǐ	v.	drive	S	8B
223	形似	xíngsì	v.	look like	G	3A
224	型号	xínghào	n.	model	S	1A
225	需求	xūqiú	n.	need	G	1A

119

（续表）

序号	生词	拼音	词性	词义	普通 G/专业 S	所属单元
226	巡回	xúnhuí	v.	tour, go the rounds	G	3A
227	迅速	xùnsù	adj.	prompt	G	1B
228	压	yā	v.	press, crush	G	6B
229	要求	yāoqiú	v.	require	G	1B
230	一维条形码（一维码）	yīwéi tiáoxíngmǎ (yīwéimǎ)	n.	one-dimensional bar code	S	9A
231	一定	yídìng	adj.	certain	G	9A
232	以及	yǐjí	conj.	and	G	7B
233	一般	yìbān	adj.	usual	G	1A
234	一起	yìqǐ	adv.	together	G	4A
235	异议	yìyì	n.	objection, disagreement	G	7A
236	易于	yìyú	v.	(of sth.) be easy (to do)	G	3B
237	应用	yìngyòng	v.	use, employ, apply	G	10A
238	用户	yònghù	n.	user, customer	G	7A
239	优惠促销	yōuhuì cùxiāo	phr.	special promotion	S	9
240	由于	yóuyú	conj.	because of, due to	G	7A
241	有效容积	yǒuxiào róngjī	phr.	effective volume	S	6B
242	于	yú	prep.	(of time/place) in, at, on	G	3A
243	与	yǔ	conj.	and, together with	G	10B
244	预约	yùyuē	v.	reserve	G	8A
245	远	yuǎn	adj.	(of time/space) far, remote	G	3B
246	阅读器	yuèdúqì	n.	reader	S	9A
247	运行	yùnxíng	v.	move	G	8A
248	再加工	zài jiāgōng	phr.	reprocess	S	2A
249	载重量	zàizhòngliàng	n.	load capacity	S	6A
250	摘果	zhāi guǒ	phr.	pick fruit	S	3A
251	摘果式拣选	zhāiguǒshì jiǎnxuǎn	phr.	DPS picking	S	3A
252	针对	zhēnduì	v.	be aimed at / targeted on / directed against	G	3A
253	整	zhěng	adj.	whole	G	5A
254	整箱补货	zhěng xiāng bǔ huò	phr.	full container load replenishment	S	5
255	之间	zhījiān	n.	space between/among things/people	G	1B
256	知	zhī	v.	know	G	10B
257	直接	zhíjiē	adj.	direct	G	2B

（续表）

序号	生词	拼音	词性	词义	普通G/专业S	所属单元
258	只	zhǐ	adv.	only	G	3A
259	只是	zhǐshì	adv.	only	G	9A
260	指	zhǐ	v.	refer to	G	6A
261	中	zhōng	n.	the inside, being within a certain range/sphere	G	7A
262	中心	zhōngxīn	n.	center	S	7A
263	重	zhòng	adj.	heavy	G	6B
264	重心	zhòngxīn	n.	center of gravity	G	6B
265	周到	zhōudào	adj.	considerate	S	1B
266	逐个	zhúgè	adv.	one by one	G	4A
267	主控站	zhǔkòngzhàn	n.	main control station	S	10
268	主要	zhǔyào	adj.	main	G	2B
269	注入站	zhùrùzhàn	n.	upload station	S	10
270	转货地	zhuǎnhuòdì	n.	place to trans-ship cargo	S	8
271	装载	zhuāngzài	v.	(of a vehicle, ship, etc.) carry, load	G	6A
272	准确	zhǔnquè	adj.	accurate	G	1B
273	着手	zhuóshǒu	v.	put one's hand to	G	1B
274	资料	zīliào	n.	data, information	S	1B
275	自动分拣系统	zìdòng fēnjiǎn xìtǒng	phr.	automatic sorting system	S	4
276	自身	zìshēn	n.	(not sb./sth.else) one's own, oneself	G	10B
277	组装	zǔzhuāng	v.	assemble	S	2A
278	最终商品	zuìzhōng shāngpǐn	phr.	final commodity final product	S	2A

视频脚本 Video Scripts

第一单元　订单处理

一、热身
A：师傅，订单处理的过程主要包括哪些步骤？

B：第一是接受订货，第二是订单确认，第三是设定订单号，第四是建立客户档案，第五是存货分配。

三、视听说
A：你知道吗？随着现代科技的发展，订货的方式逐渐由传统的人工下单、接单转变为计算机直接送收订货资料的电子订货方式了。

B：电子订货方式具有传送速度快，可靠性、准确性高，客户服务水平高等优点。

四、学以致用
大家好！今天我来给大家说说怎样完成订单录入。录入订单时先确定客户订单编号、客户名称、出货时间、拣货时间、核查时间，再输入正确的储位号码、货物名称、规格型号、货物编号以及数量。请看一个订单录入的过程，并完成练习。

第二单元　流通加工

一、热身
A：请问生产加工和流通加工的区别是什么？

B：流通加工与生产加工有明显的区别，主要表现在以下四个方面。第一，加工对象不同。流通加工的对象是商品，生产加工的对象不是最终商品而是原材料、零配件、半成品。第二，组织者不同。流通加工的组织者是商业企业或物流企业，而生产加工的组织者则是生产企业。第三，加工程度不同。流通加工大都为简单加工，而生产加工则较为复杂，技术要求高。第四，加工的目的不同。生产加工的目的是创造价值和使用价值，流通加工的目的是完善和提高商品的使用价值。

A：哦，我明白了，谢谢！

三、视听说
A：师傅，请问什么是生产加工？

B：生产加工是创造社会财富的活动和过程，是通过一定工序和方式将原材料、半成品转化为目标需求的过程。比如把棉花生产成棉布，把棉布做成衣服。

A：明白了。那么什么是流通加工呢？

B：流通加工是生产加工的辅助和补充，是生产出的物品根据需要进行包装、分割、计量、分拣、刷标志、拴标签、组装等简单作业的总称。它是物品从生产领域向消费领域流动的过程中，为了更有效地利用资源、方便用户而对物品进行的简单再加工。比如给生产出的衣服拴标签、用纸盒包装等。让我们来看看哪些是生产加工、哪些是流通加工。

自行车专卖店组装自行车	超市分割猪肉	超市中的商品捆在一起搭配销售	生产丝绸衬衫	生产火腿肠

四、学以致用
流通加工的种类很多，生活中常见的是生鲜食品的流通加工，主要有冷冻加工、分选加工、精制加工和分装加工。

1. 冷冻加工：为解决生鲜食品的保鲜、装卸、运输等问题，采取低温冷冻的加工。

2. 分选加工：对生鲜食品进行分等级挑选分类工作。

3. 精制加工：去除生鲜食品的无用部分，甚至进行切分、洗净、分装工作。

4. 分装加工：将生鲜食品按零售要求进行重新包装，例如大包装改小包装、散装改小包装等。

请为下列产品选择合适的流通加工方式。

第三单元　摘果式拣选

一、热身

A：师傅，摘果式拣选的基本流程是什么？

B：摘果式拣选就是拣货员接收到拣货任务后，针对每一个客户订单进行拣选，拣货员巡回于各个货物储位，将所需的货物依次取出，直至拣选完毕。

A：摘果式拣选的特点是什么？

B：摘果式拣选的特点是每人每次只拣选一个客户的订单，订单响应速度快，操作简单，责任明确，方便考核。当用户需求不稳定、波动较大或者用户之间需求差异较大的时候最好选用摘果式拣选。要注意的是，摘果式拣选如果不设置最后的复核环节，出错率会比较高。

A：明白了，摘果式拣选虽然简单，但需要拣货员工作认真、细致、具有责任心呀。

三、视听说

A：请问什么是电子标签拣选系统啊？

B：电子标签拣选系统以一连串装于货架格位上的电子显示装置（电子标签）取代拣货单，指示应拣取的物品及数量，辅助拣货人员作业，减少目视寻找时间。

A：电子标签拣选系统有什么特点呢？

B：电子标签拣选系统具有拣货速度快、效率高、差错率低、无纸化的作业特点，使用简单，操作人员上岗快。

四、学以致用

常用的拣选方法有摘果式拣选和播种式拣选两种。这两种方法各有利弊，具体看情况选用。当遇到以下情况时，可以选择摘果式拣选：一是订单数量多，但每张订单需要的商品种类有限；二是客户的订单需求比较紧急；三是不同客户对商品的需求差异很大。

第四单元　播种式拣选

一、热身

A：师傅，请问播种式拣选的基本流程是什么？

B：拣货员接收到客户订单后，先把一定时期的多个客户订单汇总成一批，把相同品种货物的数量进行汇总，然后把每个品种的货物拣选出来，再逐个对所有客户进行分货，最后对每个订单的商品进行复核，完成所有的配货作业。

A：播种式拣选有什么特点呢？

B：与摘果式拣选不同，播种式拣选一次可以拣选多个订单的货物，效率高，但流程确实比较复杂，是个先总后分的过程。

三、视听说

A：师傅，可以给我们介绍一下自动分拣系统吗？

B：好的。很多物流配送中心为了提高拣选效率，纷纷引进了自动分拣系统，它可以在最短的时间内从庞大的高层货架存储系统中准确找到要出库的商品所在的位置，并按所需数量从不同储位上取出，自动送到指定分拣口或特定区域，以便装车配送。

A：自动分拣系统太棒了，它有好多优点吧？

B：是的，自动分拣系统能连续、大批量地分拣货物，分拣效率高，准确率高，可以节省人力，降低货损，实现数据存储和可控管理。

四、学以致用

大家好！播种式拣选与摘果式拣选不同，播种式拣选一次可以拣选多个订单的货物，效率更高。对于品种和数量都比较多的大规模拆零拣选或者货物重合度较高的订单，都可以选择播种式拣选。请给下面这批订单选择合适的拣选方式，并做好播种式拣选的数量统计。

第五单元　补货作业

一、热身

A：师傅，补货作业的种类有哪些呀？

B：主要有三种：第一种是托盘补货，就是以托盘为单位，将地板平置堆叠保管区的货物运到地板平置堆叠动管区；第二种是整箱补货，就是由货架保管区补货到流动货架的动管区；第三种是货架上层—下层的补货，意思是保管区与动管区属于同一货架，补货时将上层保管区的货物搬至下层动管区。

三、视听说

A：请问补货作业的流程有哪些？

B：一共有6个步骤。第一步，客户订货；第二步，检查拣货区存货；第三步，当存货不足时，开始补货；第四步，找出空托盘；第五步，把装好货的托盘由保管区移至拣货区；第六步，重建存货档案并将托盘归位。

四、学以致用

大家好，我们怎样选择合适的补货方式？当货物体积大、出货量多时，应当采用托盘补货的方式，即以托盘为单位进行补货。当货品体积小且出货少的时候，需要用整箱补货的方式，即由货架保管区补货到流动货架动管区。当货物体积不大、存货量也不高的时候，应该用货架上层—下层的补货方式，就是保管区与动管区属于同一货架，补货时将上层保管区的货物搬至下层动管区。现在我就来考考大家：如果一个客户需要1000箱牛奶，可是拣货区只有10箱了，你觉得用哪种补货方式比较好呢？

第六单元　配装作业

一、热身

大家好，今天让我们了解一下配装作业的原则。原则1，充分利用车辆的有效容积和载重量。原则2，适当衬垫，防止货物损坏。原则3，禁止超重。原则4，重不压轻，大不压小。原则5，重心平衡。原则6，标签朝外。

三、视听说

A：请问货物最优配装方案是什么？

B：货物最优配装方案就是车辆的载重量和车厢容积都能被充分利用。

A：那设计货物最优配装方案需要知道什么信息呢？

B：设计货物最优配装方案需要知道4种信息：（1）2个货物的体积V1、V2；（2）货物的重量；（3）车辆的载重量；（4）车厢容积。

A：好的，谢谢。

四、学以致用

A：如果已知设计货物最优配装方案所需的4个信息，如何设计货物最优配装方案呢？

B：如果已知设计货物最优配装方案所需的4个信息分别是2个货物的体积V1、V2，计划使用车辆的载重量A，车厢容积B，用公式计算出两个货物的重量W1和W2就行了。

计算公式：

$$\begin{cases} W1+W2=A \\ V1*W1+V2*W2=B \end{cases}$$

举个例子：

某配送中心需配送水泥和玻璃两种货物，V1 水泥是 2m³/t，V2 玻璃是 1m³/t，车辆的载重量A是10t，车厢容积 B 是 15m³，请问最优配装方案是什么？水泥的重量 W1 是多少？玻璃的重量 W2 是多少？

用公式计算得出最优配装方案：水泥的重量 W1 是 5t，玻璃的重量 W2 是 5t。

现在我来考考你：

某配送中心某次需配送牛奶和苹果两种货物，牛奶的体积 V1 是 2m³/t，苹果的体积 V2 是 1m³/t，计划使用车辆的载重量 A 是 15t，车厢容积 B 是 25m³。试问牛奶的重量 W1 是多少？苹果的重量 W2 是多少？

第七单元　退货作业

一、热身

大家好，今天让我们了解一下退货的原因。原因 1，有质量问题。原因 2，搬运中损坏。原因 3，商品过期，例如：面包是 2021 年 5 月 3 日生产的，只能存放 3 天，那么 2021 年 5 月 7 日吃的时候就过期了。原因 4，次品回收。

三、视听说

今天我们一起了解拒绝客户退货要求的几种情况。

情况 1：超过规定退货时间。例如：2021 年 5 月 10 日购买了一台电视机，退货时间是一个月以内，那么一个月内有问题的话可以退货，所以 2021 年 6 月 10 日之前都可以退货。但是，2021 年 6 月 10 日之后就不可以退货了。

情况 2：所退商品数量不够，外观受损。

情况 3：发票、收据丢失。

四、学以致用

A：请问退货作业的流程有哪些？

B：一共有 5 个步骤。

　　第一步，退货验收作业：退货收货员核对退货名称、数量、规格、保持期等信息。

　　第二步，退货整理作业：将验收好的货品按照供应商、生产日期、货品的状态分类整理，装入物流箱中。

　　第三步，良品入库作业：将良品分类整理好，交入库上架员验收，然后人工上架，并登记货卡。

　　第四步，拒收退作业：对于不符合退货条件的货品，由配送员退给客户并附带拒收退原因说明。

　　第五步，不良品退货作业：不良品移交供应商，供应商审核退货。

第八单元　运输调度

一、热身

A：运输调度主要需要做什么啊？

B：第一，了解用车信息。第二，调度员根据了解的用车信息合理安排车辆。第三，监控车辆行驶。

A：用车信息包括哪些啊？

B：包括：1.转货地；2.时间；3.联系人；4.车辆要求。

A：如何监控车辆行驶？

B：车上安装了一些设备和系统进行监控，包括车辆管理系统、行程记录仪、GPS 导航仪、安全行驶报警系统。

A：好的，明白了，谢谢。

三、视听说

大家好，今天让我们了解一下车辆管理系统的功能。

功能 1：可以实时监控每辆车的运行轨迹。通过车辆管理系统可以知道任何时间点车辆所在的位置。

功能 2：运输量大的时候，可以通过系统提前预约车辆。例如，如果 10 号需要用车，可以提前在车辆管理系统中输入日期，这样就可以确保当天有车。

功能 3：系统可以自动向承运商发送车辆预约提醒。例如，在车辆管理系统中输入 10 号要用车，系统在 9 号会提示您。

四、学以致用

A：请问运输调度的流程有哪些？

B：一共有5个步骤：第一步，客户预约；第二步，调度员了解用车信息；第三步，调度员根据了解的用车信息合理安排车辆；第四步，调度员监控车辆行驶；第五步，货物交货处理。

第九单元　条码技术

一、热身

A：一维条形码与二维码分别用于什么地方呢？

B：一维条形码可用于食品、饮料、药品等商品上，消费者因商品条码购物更方便。常见的二维码是近几年来移动设备上超流行的一种编码方式，主要有以下功能：

1. 防伪溯源：用户扫码即可查看生产地，同时后台可以获取最终消费地。
2. 优惠促销：用户扫码下载电子优惠券、抽奖。
3. 广告推送：用户扫码直接浏览商家推送的视频、音频广告。
4. 手机支付：扫描商品二维码，通过银行或第三方支付提供的手机端通道完成支付。
5. 信息获取：如名片、地图、WIFI密码、资料等。

三、视听说

A：一维条形码有什么特性呢？

B：数据容量较小，30个字符左右，只能包含字母和数字，尺寸较大，条形码损坏后就不能读取信息了。

A：那二维码呢？

B：二维码与一维条形码相比有明显的优势：数据容量更大，没有字母、数字的限制，尺寸小，具有抗损毁能力。

四、学以致用

大家好！今天我来给大家说说怎样生成一个二维码。步骤一：打开二维码生成器。步骤二：输入货品入库信息、商品基本信息，包括商品名称、价格、厂家、图片等。步骤三：挑选形状、颜色等。步骤四：点击完成。一个二维码就生成了，让我们动手做一个吧。

第十单元　全球定位系统（GPS）

一、热身

A：GPS有哪几部分构成？

B：主要包括三大部分：空间部分——GPS卫星星座，地面控制部分——地面监控系统，用户部分——GPS信号接收机。

三、视听说

A：GPS有哪些应用领域？

B：GPS的应用领域无所不在，比如：利用GPS技术可以实时进行车辆定位，并任意放大、缩小、还原、换图；车载GPS可以让你跟着导航前往目的地；GPS还能进行宠物跟踪；跟踪手环利用GPS可以进行人物定位；等等。

四、学以致用

A：我想开车从市民中心前往南京博物院，可我不知道路线怎么办呀？

B：你可以打开手机GPS，然后打开手机地图，输入起点为"市民中心"，终点为"南京博物院"，点击"开始导航"，跟着导航的路线开车就可以啦。

参考答案 Reference Answers

第一单元

一、热身

1. ①B ②D ③A ④C

2. E C B A D

三、视听说

B C F H

四、学以致用

①C ②E ③A ④D ⑤B

第二单元

一、热身

1. ①C ②D ③B ④A

2. 生产加工的特征：B D F G 流通加工的特征：A C E H

三、视听说

生产加工：D E 流通加工：A B C

四、学以致用

①A ②D ③C ④B

第三单元

一、热身

1. ①B ②C ③A ④D

2. B A C

三、视听说

A D E F

四、学以致用

A B D

第四单元

一、热身

1. ①C ②A ③D ④B

2. C A B

三、视听说

A C E F G H

四、学以致用

拣选决策（打"√"）picking decision (×)			播种式拣选汇总 DAS picking summary	
订单 orders	摘果式拣选 DPS picking	播种式拣选 DAS picking	货物名称 name of goods	数量 quantity
订单 1		√	《物流管理》	130
订单 2		√	《仓储管理》	140
订单 3		√	《配送管理》	150
订单 4		√	《运输管理》	120
订单 5	√		《汉语》	15
订单 6		√	《英语》	15
			《法语》	15

第五单元

一、热身

1. ① B ② A ③ D ④ C
2. ① C ② B ③ A

三、视听说

⑥ ④ ② ① ③ ⑤

四、学以致用

A

第六单元

一、热身

1. ① A ② B ③ C ④ D
2. ① C ② A ③ D ④ B ⑤ F ⑥ E

三、视听说

A C D F

四、学以致用

牛奶的重量是 5t，苹果的重量是 10t。

第七单元

一、热身

1. ① A ② D ③ C ④ B
2. 看视频

① B ② D ③ A ④ C

三、视听说

① A ② C ③ B

四、学以致用

③ ⑤ ① ④ ②

第八单元

一、热身

1. ①D ②C ③B ④A
2. ①D ②A ③C ④B

三、视听说

①B ②C ③A

四、学以致用

⑤ ④ ② ① ③

第九单元

一、热身

1. ①B ②C ③D ④A
2. A B D E F

三、视听说

一维条形码的特性：C F G
二维条形码的特性：A B D E

四、学以致用

A D B C

第十单元

一、热身

1. ①B ②C ③A
2.

GPS 的组成

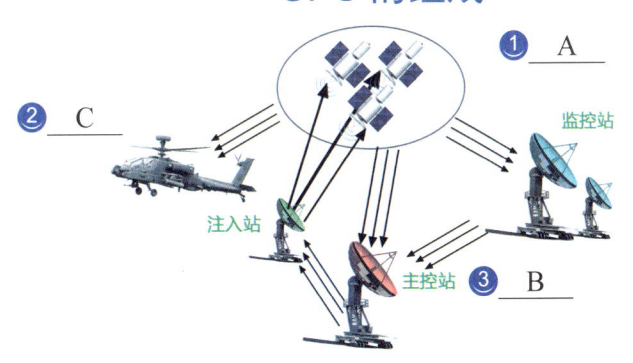

① A _____
② C _____ 监控站
注入站
主控站
③ B _____

三、视听说

①D ②B ③A ④C

四、学以致用

B A C